The Missing Voice

SANDI ASHLEY

WRITINGS

BY

MOTHERS

OF

INCEST

VICTIMS

KENDALL/HUNT PUBLISHING COMPANY
2460 Kerper Boulevard   P.O. Box 539   Dubuque, Iowa 52004-0539

Contents

(Names and situations have been altered to protect the identities of the people described in this book)

Acknowledgments

First and foremost, I wish to acknowledge all of the mothers of sexual abuse survivors who have honored me by sharing their lives, their pain, and their growth with me. This book is by them and for them and others suffering from the effects of sexual assault.

There are many others I wish to thank for their contribution to this work: My husband, David Ashley, and my friend, Sue Barton, MSW, who willingly provided whatever was needed at the time, from creative ideas to editorial assistance to moral support; Kathleen Hayden, MSW; Ron Silvers, M.Ed.; and Laurie Ekanger who contributed professional and editorial expertise for my chapter; Rick Graetz and Mark Thompson who helped me with the ins and outs of the publishing world; our typist who typed and copied at odd hours of the day and night to meet deadlines; and all of my friends and fellow professionals who have encouraged and challenged me throughout my professional career.

TO THOSE WHO HAVE SURVIVED
THE VIOLENCE OF SEXUAL ABUSE

The Freight Train

"It's like a freight train roars through your life and leaves a huge hole. Everything is shattered . . . ," I said to the woman sitting in my office. She nodded, tears rolling down her cheeks. She was still in shock from hearing that her husband, who she needed and trusted, and her son, who she cherished and felt so proud of, had sexually molested her daughter.

As we sat together, I could see the memories and the feelings from the last few days cross her face. First came the call from the social worker—confusing. "I wonder what she wants me for?" Then the meeting with the social worker. "Your daughter told a school counselor that your husband and your son . . ." Then the freight train that keeps roaring and roaring, and the shattering in her head that won't stop.

There is so much shock, numbness, pain, anger, disbelief. "It is true—no! It can't be!! Who are these people I love and thought I knew? Who am I? Why did they do it? Is she all right? Why couldn't she tell me?" The pain comes and comes in waves, almost drowning her. Then the shame and guilt. "I need to function and take care of things—my family, my job, my life! But I can't. I'm shattered, so ashamed and so alone. What happened? What does it mean? Is this all my fault?" Question after screaming question. Now a visit to a therapist who seems to understand this unfathomable thing, who offers hope, and who says I am not alone.

The Missing Voice is written by women who have been torn apart by incest committed by people they love against people they love. Some of them suffered the agony of sexual abuse as children by people they loved, trusted, and depended on for guidance, care and role modeling. They swore it would never happen in their own families, to their own children, but somehow, it did.

The idea for this book came from a therapy group for women whose sons and/or husbands molested their children.[1] The group began in 1985 when the sex offender treatment program in our community, which serves much of Western Montana, added therapy groups for victim/survivors and wife/mothers.

---

1. We recognize that women also perpetuate sexual offenses, and that boys are also victimized. However, in our group, the offenders were male and the victims were female. Therefore, these terms will be used to preserve clarity.

When another therapist and I were planning the wife/mother group, we anticipated that the women would resist coming to the group. We thought they would take months to open up, to share themselves, and to relate their individual experiences. We were half right. It was hard for them to come the first time. They feared judgment, blame and criticism. They feared being disloyal to the offender and the victim by exposing the family secret. They feared touching their pain. They feared intensely, without knowing all the reasons why.

When they came, they were relieved to find a safe place—a place where they were not judged, a place where they were not alone, a place where people cared and understood. The group was a place where they could begin to understand themselves and the incest. They could begin the process of healing and rebuilding. The group was uniquely for them, and it could be whatever they wanted or needed it to be. The group bonded women from different walks of life as they shared their common journey. At first the group was scheduled once every other week. At the first meeting, group members asked to meet weekly because they were so hungry for the sharing and support the group provided.

After a year and a half of sharing their life stories, fears, hopes and pain; of exploring personal strengths and working through personal shortcomings, issues, and mistakes; of supporting each other through crises such as disclosures of more abuse, problems of parenting traumatized children, court dates, and unemployment; and of celebrating successes, birthdays, and sobriety anniversaries, the idea for this book began to emerge. The group was filling a critical need for these women. Each of their stories had much to say to women out there alone suffering the pain of incest. They wanted to reach out to each of them. They wanted to have some good come from the hell they were working through.

The women and I formed a separate volunteer group to start work on this book and to help other wife/mothers. The women in this group work with the local criminal justice/child protective system for more effective services for incest families. They advocate for more informed and respectful coverage by the news media. They talk to community groups and provide crisis intervention services to women who discover that incest has occurred in their families. They speak to groups of offenders, including those that are incarcerated, about the effects of sexually abusive behavior.

When we began to work on this book, the women were dedicated but frightened. They voiced their questions: ''Can I really write all of this? What will my family think? What will it be like to open up all of those feelings again? Will readers understand, or will they be repelled by the raw, stark reality of sexual assault within a family?''

They called a special meeting to overcome their fears and to brainstorm their purpose. Coffee, doughnuts, blue jeans, Saturday morning. Everyone was talking excitedly. ''Sorry I'm late. You won't believe who called! My daughter's father she hasn't seen since birth. She wrote to him a few weeks ago, and she is thrilled!'' ''Great! Glad you're here. Let's get started.''

They asked themselves two questions: ''Who do we want to reach? What do we want to tell them?'' ''We want to enlighten therapists and social workers. They don't understand. So many of us faced judgments and condemnation that made things worse. We want to help educate the general public on the problem of incest and help them understand. This is one way we can work toward more effective prevention and intervention. If more people understand, the stigma and isolation will be reduced. Maybe then it will be easier for incest families to disclose the secret and to seek help from professionals and support from friends.''

''We want to reach other wife/mothers who don't have a group or a therapist to help her and to ease her loneliness. It is so lonely at first and later during the inevitable bad times. You know, this isn't something you share with your neighbor over a cup of coffee. This is an important point: We want to offer her courage and hope. Maybe reading about one of our journeys will help her move forward on hers. Maybe it will help her realize that her feelings aren't crazy. Maybe it will give her the strength to look at herself, to begin to value herself, and to make the changes she wants to make.''

''What else?''

''We have a message for women who live in families that look fine, but there is a vague sense that something may be wrong in their families.''

''Does something seem unusual in the relationship between your husband or son and your daughter, either excessive closeness or fear and anger? Does your daughter seem clingy, angry, or depressed, or is she experiencing health, school or peer problems? Do you find yourself withdrawing from your family? Is your husband a Dr. Jekyll/Mr. Hyde? If you are answering yes to these questions—as horrifying as it may seem that the man you chose to love, trust and commit your life to, or that the son you raised is a sex offender—consider incest!''

''We want to touch children and adults traumatized by incest. Many times wife/mothers, because of their own trauma, respond inappropriately and insensitively to their children before and during the disclosure. We hope when they read this some of that hurt can be healed.''

''What else?'' ''We want the offenders to know how it felt to live in this family, and how it feels to be their wife or mother. We want them to hear the pain, betrayal, and fear. We want them to know what they did to our self-esteem. We want them to know that their power over us is gone. We are now strong enough to understand and take responsibility for our part—the not seeing, the excusing, the enabling, and tolerating the intolerable. We no longer take responsibility for their abusiveness.''

"Finally we want to tell it how it really is—about ourselves, our families, and the incest. The good, the bad and the ugly. No minimizing. We will change the names and identifying circumstances to protect our children. We don't want them to suffer if someone doesn't understand. This is their story, too, and it is important to respect that. But it is healing to break the silence, to be honest, and to be real. This is one way we can try to interrupt the devastating cycle of sexual abuse."

After the brainstorming session, the women continued to meet. They took turns reading what they had written. Tears were shed. Hugs were gratefully received. It was hard, but healing, to feel it all again. Encouragement was passed around when a painful part hit. Each story is unique and brings its own messages, adding its part to the overall picture. As the book progressed, more excitement spread through the group. "We're doing it! It's really happening! The process of writing is so good for us. We hope it's half as good for the readers!"

In the Beginning—The Disclosure of the Incest

What does a wife/mother feel when she first hears that her child has been molested? Shock and denial. "No way!! I can't believe this is happening. It's a nightmare. I would give anything to be able to wake up! It's like I've left my body and I'm watching all of this happen from far away. How could he? He couldn't have!! Why didn't she tell me? If it happened, she would have." Shock, then denial. Back and forth. Then the minimization. "It can't be as bad as they say." She may begin to accept it intellectually but stays disconnected from the emotional impact.

Confusion abounds. She feels confused by the child protective/legal system. "Does this mean I have to get divorced? Will I lose my child? What is happening? What is going to happen?" She is confused by the usual differences in accounts given by her child and the offender. "Who can I believe? Who is lying? Why? How can this fit with the way I know my husband, my child, and my family? What is wrong with me? How could this have happened without my knowledge?" She goes searching through the past for evidence, bits, clues.

For some women, the pieces begin to fall into place. She remembers when the offender's behavior was strange, unexplainable. She remembers feelings, like feeling left out when she was with her husband and child, or that funny feeling in her stomach that something undefinable was wrong and strange. In some ways, the unfathomable is beginning to make sense. Emotionally, it feels crazy—a big tangle of emotions, possible and impossible at the same time, and just plain crazy. It is scary to feel so crazy.

If the wife/mother was sexually victimized as a child, discovering her child's victimization is a double trauma. In addition to experiencing all of the wife/mother feelings, she is overwhelmed by the unresolved memories, pain, confusion, anger, fear, guilt and shame from her own victimization. All of the trauma she spent years burying is suddenly hitting her with the force that only buried emotions can produce. All of the messages from her victimization seem to be coming true. "You are worthless. You never do anything right. You are incapable of anything, and responsible for everything. You are bad." These messages and the feelings of worthlessness, helplessness, and hopelessness are indescribably intense for these women.

As time goes along, the wife/mother has many other emotions to work through. She needs to find the safety to feel and express the anger at him, at herself, and (although it seems irrational and unacceptable after all she has gone through) at her child. She usually experiences intense guilt over feeling angry with her child, and may have great difficulty working through it. This anger may be directed at the child for not telling her, or it may be directed at the child in her other role, as husband's lover. This anger may actually be anger at the offender or from her own childhood that is displaced on the child.

If she blames herself for her own victimization, she may also blame her child for her victimization. Intellectually, she may understand why the child couldn't tell and that the "other role" is not the child's fault. But she still feels angry. Her dream of having a beautiful, happy, respected, nice family has been shattered, and she is angry and hurt. Sometimes what she experiences as anger is actually a mix of anger, hurt, and fear. These feelings are often displaced from the family members to the system. This is a safer way for some women to feel it and express it. It is important for her ultimately to work through the displacement, and to deal with her anger directly with her family members.

Throughout all of this, there is the need to cope. She needs to get to work, to get the kids to school, to get out of bed each morning. She wants to try to act normal. If she can act normal, maybe it is proof that she is still sane, and that the whole world isn't as crazy as it feels. Everything is falling apart on the inside. She tries desperately to keep it as together as possible on the outside. Besides, the family needs to eat, and the bills need to be paid. Possibly, if she can act normal, not everyone will know about her shame.

There is even more confusion. She holds strong, conflicting feelings for both the offender and her child. Most likely she deeply loves and is intensely angry with both of them. She is jealous of the sexual (and possibly emotional) relationship they had that she was denied. It is hard to sort this all out. She wants to support both of them, despite her angry feelings. It feels as if she has to choose between them. Her loyalty is torn, and it is ripping her apart. Because of her emotional trauma, it may be difficult for her to truly support either of them.

She is experiencing deep feelings of isolation. She feels such shame. "This is the worst thing that could happen. Incest doesn't happen in respectable families where people are okay. Who will understand? I don't even understand!" The people she has talked to so far don't seem supportive. Either it is people in the system asking her to do things, or people saying, "How can you care at all about the SOB?," or "He is such a wonderful man. He couldn't have done it. Stick with him." It seems like no one can understand what she is going through, and like no one has faced this before. She is all alone at a time of great need. She is cut off from the support system she might have had if the issue were different.

Depression sets in. Sometimes it is tears. They always seem to come at the wrong time, and it feels like they won't stop. Sometimes it is numbness. Everything feels wooden. Often sleeping and eating habits are disrupted. It is hard to concentrate. It is hard to simply be here in reality. It is hard to find the energy to do even the smallest things.

The fear is everywhere. There is fear of the unknown, such as the workings of the system and what that process will require of her. There is fear of failing to cope with practical issues such as finances and parenting children who are dealing with their own trauma. There is fear of the huge, intense feelings of anger and pain that are right under the surface. There is fear that she is bad, and that her "badness" somehow caused all of this to happen. There is fear that something else just as unexpected could happen any-time.

The combination of fear and depression is immobilizing. She has no energy to act, and great fear that if she does act she will do something wrong and cause more problems. More problems mean more overwhelming feelings. She may try to block her feelings in an attempt to cope, but this, too, takes energy and contributes to immobilization.

The guilt is there. "It is my fault. I wasn't good enough in bed so he turned to her. I was too fat or too bitchy. It is my fault. I didn't protect my child." The guilt feelings are especially intense if her daughter previously tried to tell her about the incest. Some of the guilt is rational and some is not. Sometimes it is easier to feel the irrational guilt than to feel the anger, fear and helplessness that exist in a world where incest occurs. Sometimes it is easier to feel the irrational guilt than to sort out and face her role and responsibility as the mother of the victim.

Some wife/mothers feel guilty "by association." They think that because they have a relationship with a sex offender that they somehow share in his guilt and responsibility for offending. They also fear that their children, friends, and community will blame them because of their association with the offender. Often they feel blamed by the child protective/criminal justice system.

The betrayal is insidious. When a person discovers that their truest and most precious reality is a lie, it is devastating. When she experiences this, the wife/mother massively loses trust in herself and in her ability to accurately discern and respond to reality. Trust is also lost in others. She feels threatened, suspicious, insecure. Her self-image is shattered. She is not who she thought she was, and doesn't know who she is. Her self-esteem plunges. She fears that who she is is bad. She can't connect with her strengths and assets. All of this contributes to her isolation. Who can she confide in? Who can she trust? Will she just find another offender?

The Journey After Disclosure

One of the big questions facing a wife/mother is: "How could incest happen in my family without my knowledge?" Most of the wife/mothers are aware of problems in their families but are not aware of the incest. Often this wife/mother attributes the problems she is aware of to other family problems, such as alcoholism or adjusting to a step-family situation, or she attributes the problems to a difficulty her husband is dealing with, such as job stress or disability. She may also attribute them to individual issues facing her child such as hyperactivity, learning problems, or poor peer relationships. She has a vague sense, or maybe even a clear idea, that there is a problem, but she has not identified the problem as incest.

Her inability to identify the problem as incest may stem from at least two sources. One is denial. Many times it is hard to imagine that the man she chooses to spend her life with could sexually assault his child, or that the son she raised could sexually assault his sister. It can be equally hard to believe that the child wouldn't tell her.

Considering the possibility of incest in her family would force her to make major, difficult changes in her beliefs and feelings about herself as a wife, mother, woman, and person. These roles are the most crucial, personal, intimate ones she has. Tough questions face her: "Can't I satisfy my husband sexually and emotionally? What is wrong with me that I would marry or raise a sex offender? What kind of parent am I? What is wrong with me that I didn't protect my child? Why couldn't she come to me? Am I weak, inadequate, evil, unfortunate?"

Considering the possibility of incest also forces her to change her beliefs and feelings about the people closest to her. She could be left with intense, overwhelming feelings of hurt, anger, betrayal, guilt, and shame. More tough questions face her: "Who is this man I thought I knew? Who is this son I raised from birth? Why didn't I see this side of him?"

Finally she is forced to make changes in how she and the rest of the family members function emotionally and financially. She may have to face losing her husband and becoming a single parent. She may have to deal with her child's removal from the home. She may have to intimately confront and relate emotionally with her husband and her child. Although she probably does not know all of this, she senses that considering the possibility of incest in her family would be devastating, and require changes she fears she can't make, and emotional resources she fears she doesn't have. The possibility of incest doesn't even enter her mind or is quickly pushed aside if it does.

The second reason she may not be aware of incest is because the offender and possibly the victim are both working hard to keep it from her. The offender, for obvious reasons, does not want her to know. The victim may wish to protect her mother from the pain it would cause her. She may fear her mother's anger, especially if the offender has made her feel responsible for the abuse. Or she may be too afraid to tell because of threats made by the offender such as, "If you tell your mother, it will kill her," or "I will kill you," or "I will go to prison and the whole family will suffer and it will be your fault." These threats are not made lightly, and the child takes them very seriously.

Other questions facing the wife/mother are: "Why didn't I do something? Why did I stay? Even if I didn't know about the incest, I knew there were problems." This wife/mother lives in great fear. Her husband is a violent, domineering person. She is afraid if she asks questions, attempts to make changes or (God forbid!) leaves her husband, it will only make things worse. He might harm her or their children even more. The longer she stays, the more she fears, the more power she gives him, and the more her self-confidence and courage are eroded. Choices that were once open to her, such as demanding that they seek counseling, or leaving, now seem impossible. She may also fear having to cope with the loneliness and responsibilities of being on her own.

In other situations, the husband appears to be a nice guy—manipulative, but nice. There is not a closeness in the marriage and things feel wrong, but he is so nice and good, probably even a prominent church or community leader. In this situation, the wife/mother has difficulty trusting and acting on her internal sense that something is wrong. She probably learned in her birth family that she couldn't trust her own feelings, so it doesn't occur to her to trust them now. Externally, it all looks so right.

She may also stay in the family and maintain the status quo out of a sense of duty and because of her own definition of her role as a wife. This woman believes deeply that divorce is wrong, and it is her place to support her husband, ease his difficulties, and smooth over his problems and the family stresses. She needs to make the best of things—in good times and in bad, "Until death us do part." She must make a success of the marriage even if it means she makes sacrifices. These values may have been instilled by her church and her family from an early age. This makes it difficult for her to bring up problems and take independent action.

Many times the wife/mother feels that the marriage relationship is a good one in the beginning. She loves this man, and he truly seems to be a considerate, caring person. Then things begin to change, but they change gradually, just a little tiny bit each day. She doesn't really notice the change or realize how bad things have become. Again, it may all look fine on the outside. Friends may have no idea anything is wrong. The wife/mother believes that her problems are no worse than anyone else's, and after all, life isn't perfect. Therefore, she continues to make the best of things. She remains unaware of how serious the problems are, and that one of the problems is incest. It is like the proverbial frog in the pot. If a frog jumps into a pot of boiling water, he jumps out. If he jumps into a pot of cool water and the heat is slowly turned up, he doesn't notice the change or perceive the danger. Soon, he is cooked.

It may also be hard for her to take effective action when the offender is her son. Usually juvenile sex offenders are exhibiting behavior and emotional problems before the incest part of their problems has been identified. The wife/mother may have difficulty intervening because her son may be "beyond the control of parents." He may be old enough, strong enough, powerful enough, and troubled enough to resist parental rules and controls. If he is younger or more compliant, the wife/mother may feel that his problems are normal, a stage he is going through and will outgrow. She does not realize how serious his problems are. Some women do seek help for their children through school or private counselors. Sometimes the incest is still not discovered, or is minimized by the professional and inadequately resolved. When this happens, the incest usually starts again.

The women writing this book experienced many of these feelings and considered these questions. In group therapy, they gained the courage to face the incest and to deal with the trauma. They discovered the effects of the incest on their self-esteem, body image, sexuality, and ability to trust and feel safe in the world. They learned to reconnect with their feelings and to express them constructively. They bravely worked through the pain from their own childhoods and found some of the love and support that was there. They diligently explored their birth family legacy to rework the negative dynamics controlling their lives and to capitalize on the positive messages they received. They looked at their personal issues, defenses, needs, and strengths. They began to resolve their role in the incestuous family dynamics. They learned about appropriate roles and boundaries, and clear, honest communication. They developed assertiveness skills. They became more independent. They began to stop enabling and to experience love, trust and intimacy in relationships. They learned how to parent more effectively.

They faced crises such as separation from their children and/or husband, unemployment, being forced to accept public assistance, and deciding to divorce. Some of them had to fight for sole custody of their children. Some had to help their children through suicidal and behavior problem periods. Some had to support their children through court proceedings. Some worked closely with the offenders as they dealt with difficult issues and feelings in their treatment. Sometimes it felt overwhelming—resolving their relationships with their husbands, developing their relationships with their children who were victimized, meeting the needs of their other children, and nurturing their own growth. Through it all, each woman began to build a valuable sense of self, family relationships and coping skills. It is a big job. In many ways, it is a lifelong process. They are on the road.

As you read their stories, you will see that this road has its ups and downs. Many of these women continue to deal with the effects of the incest and the years the family functioned as an incestuous family. Some of the women strive to build on the personal changes they made in therapy. Some of them work diligently to maintain intimate, constructive relationships with their husbands. Some of them need to provide continued extra emotional support to the victim/survivors. In other instances, they are working in therapy with children who were not direct victims of the incest but suffered from the incestuous family dysfunction. But their lives are different. They don't deny the problems as they once did. They have more skills to deal with it than they once did.

I have been fortunate enough to know each of these women. They have trusted me to walk a ways with them on their journey. They have shared their secrets, pain, and darkness. They have shared their joys, successes, and progress. They are courageous, wonderful, beautiful, and very human. Their hope is mine: that their stories will touch you and bring you the light of understanding, hope, caring and companionship.

A Perspective for Those Who Want to Know More

This book and these women are part of lifting the shroud of silence that has surrounded the occurrence of incest for decades. Many efforts are being made to end the ignorance, minimizing, and distortion of the problem of incest. Victim/survivors are speaking out on television, and publishing their stories. Treatment programs for victims and offenders are springing up around the country. Many books and articles are available to train therapists in the dynamics and treatment of incestuous families. Prevention programs are a part of the curriculum in many school districts.

However, the wife/mother is often ignored. Little is written about her, for her, or by her. Treatment programs either offer nothing for her or they ask for her participation as support for the offender or the victim without recognizing and treating her needs. Commonly the child protective system intervenes for the victim, and the criminal justice system seeks appropriate intervention for the offender. Too often, the wife/mother is left unsupported, frightened, bewildered, and alone. She feels responsible for the emotional health of her family, but her sense of confidence about herself as a mother and wife is severely shaken. She feels deeply threatened by so many outsiders getting involved in her family. She becomes immobilized—lacking the skills and emotional resources to deal with this crisis in her life and having nowhere to turn for help. But she is important. Her story is important. She is "The Missing Voice."

The wife/mother has not been completely ignored in the literature. However, she has traditionally been portrayed in a limited, derogatory way, and has even been held responsible for her husband's sexually abusive behavior! She has been called a "silent partner" in the incest (Forward and Buck, 1979). She has been accused of knowing about the incest, consciously or unconsciously. She has been characterized as contributing to the incest either by neglecting her husband and her daughter, or by offering her daughter to her husband as a surrogate wife/mother. She has been described as passive, dependent, cold and withdrawn.

It is difficult for a woman to trust and work with professionals who perceive her from this viewpoint and fail to see her strengths, her efforts, and her pain. She needs empathy, not judgment, and should seek out professionals who understand her and her position.

The literature accurately describes a small minority of wife/mothers. However, it is incomplete, negative, and stated too strongly to fit most women in incestuous families. My experience, like that of many other professionals[2] is that very few of these women "offer their daughters to their husbands as surrogate wife/mothers." They are not "silent partners" in the incest, and honestly deny any knowledge of it. They are not responsible for the offender's behavior. Most of them deeply love their children and their husbands, and strive for a good family life. They are capable of offering nurturing, affection, warmth, and emotional presence to their family members, although the amount may be limited by their own unmet needs and pain. They are using all of the tools they have to be effective wives and parents in their families. Many of them have made courageous efforts to provide for their children's emotional and developmental needs. Many of them are strongly committed to creating a better family life for their children than they had. Many of them possess important strengths and values that they work to pass on to their children.

Many wife/mothers are hurt by the pain and trauma of their own life experiences. As a result, many of them suffer from low self-esteem, underdeveloped self-concepts, and limited self-confidence. Some are withdrawn and have trouble trusting themselves or others. Some have limited social and parenting skills. It is hard for them to provide emotional resources for their children because emotional resources weren't there when they were children.

Some have learned to deal with their pain by going through life hidden behind a tough shell. Others deny and distort reality so it doesn't hurt so much. Others disconnect from all of their feelings to try not to feel the pain. Others have a lifetime worth of hurt and anger stored inside. Some feel chronically depressed. Some have difficulty being assertive and taking independent action. It is hard to stand up for yourself when you feel worthless. Some are more assertive and put their energy into interests or careers outside the family where they are successful and get some of their needs met. Some are ambivalent. They want to assert themselves but fear independent action. They want to be close and loving, but fear the potential hurt in intimacy. Some expect failure and this expectation creates a self-fulfilling prophecy. Some are angry to the point of blaming their husbands or themselves for everything. A sense of realistic responsibility is lost.

No wife/mother has to deal with all of these issues. Each one is a unique individual who has developed her own way of coping with her life experience. The characteristics she has are often part of her legacy from her birth family. They are intensified by living as part of an incestuous family.

The family the wife/mother lives in is often dynamically similar to the family she was raised in. The characteristics she developed to cope in her birth family partially determine her choice of mate and her parenting style. This puts her at risk to marry or raise an offender, and to continue to reenact the dynamics of her birth family. The fam-

2. See Appendix, page 13.

ily of origin for a majority of these women is characterized by physical, emotional, or sexual abuse, neglect, alcoholism, and/or parental absence or mental illness. And the hurtful abuse/neglect cycle rolls on . . .

These families usually have confused roles, and poorly defined boundaries. Child is also adult—as a sexual partner and maybe performing parental housekeeping and emotional duties. Who is mother? Who is wife? The dual sexual relationship makes someone feel like "the other woman." Does the child have the opportunity to be a child? Happy? Cared for? To function effectively, families need a boundary where sex occurs only among the adults, where parents are responsible caretakers for their children, and where children have an opportunity to put their energy into their own growth and development instead of into pseudo-adult behavior.

The incest secret builds walls between family members. The lack of boundaries results in intrusiveness between family members. Family members often lack appropriate privacy. People are separate in ways they need to be close and, simultaneously, close in ways they need to be separate. They don't have the permission or ability to say no. This makes it difficult for children to develop an adequate identity, and to ultimately separate from the family and function as responsible adults. The emotional climate of the family is tinged with fear, guilt, anger, and sadness. Parents fail to model appropriate expression of needs and feelings. The most glaring example of this is engaging in a sexually abusive relationship with a child to express anger, insecurity and/or a need for intimacy. Therefore, the children grow up disconnected from and afraid of their feelings. They are unable to use the information and energy from their feelings to guide them in life.

Communication is not clear, direct, or easily understood in the family. Instead, communication between parents is often routed through one of the children. "You understand Dad. You go talk to him." Issues that need to be talked about often aren't brought up. If they are, a resolution is not reached. A lot of the communication contains double or hidden messages which are confusing and sometimes frightening. Therefore, relationships are less open, trusting and safe.

All of these family dynamics affect everyone in the family: the offender, the wife/mother, the victim/survivor, and the other children. The family dynamics can be as damaging to its members as the actual incest.

Is the wife/mother a victim of the sexual abuse of her child? In many ways, the answer is yes. Just as she brought her personality characteristics to the marriage, her husband brought his, including his sex offender characteristics. Many offenders have committed sexual offenses or engaged in pre-offense behavior (e.g. reading child pornography) prior to their relationships with the wife/mothers. She is not responsible for his behavior, and his sexual offending is not her fault. Many people have personality characteristics similar to the wife/mother's, and their children aren't victimized by incest. She may be limited in some ways, but she is not responsible for her husband's sexually abusive behavior.

If the offender is her son, the issue is more complex. The wife/mother is responsible for the parenting she provided (or failed to provide), and for the quality of the relationship she developed with her child. She is responsible for providing a safe home for him where he feels loved and valued. She is responsible for providing the guidance and role modeling he needs to grow, develop, and learn to express his emotions and needs appropriately, not abusively. Obviously, the child's father shares equally in these responsibilities. Ultimately, the son must take responsibility for his behavior and the choices he makes, particularly as he grows older.

Clearly the wife/mother is responsible for her behavior and her choices. She is one of two adults responsible for the functioning of the marriage and the family so that all members, including her husband and herself, are nurtured. She is one of two adults responsible for raising the children. She is responsible for finding ways to love and understand herself, to heal and cope with the effects of her dysfunctional childhood. She is responsible for how she manages her life.

The writers of this book are working to understand, forgive, and love themselves; to accept their rightful responsibility; and to do what they can to break the abuse/neglect cycle. Their stories will tell you about who they are, where they came from, choices they made, and the forces that dictated their lives. They are stories of suffering, courage, hope, and love. They will tell you about the pain of the freight train and the growth and healing afterwards.

Please contact us if you have any questions. If you need assistance in locating resources, please call your local or state mental health center, social services department, rape crisis center, or local crisis clinic.

Sandi Ashley, Licensed Professional Counselor
48 Medical Park Dr.
Helena, Montana 59601 (406) 449–3880

References

Forward, Susan and Buck, Craig. Betrayal of Innocence: Incest and Its Devastation. Penguin Books, 1978.

Appendix

Butler, Sandra. The Conspiracy of Silence: The Trauma of Incest. Volcano Press, 1985.
Byerly, Carolyn. The Mother's Book: How to Survive the Incest of Your Child. Kendall/Hunt Publishing Co., 1985.
Maltz, Wendy and Holman, Beverly. Incest and Sexuality: A Guide to Understanding and Healing. Lexington Books, 1987.
Sgroi, Suzanne. Handbook of Clinical Intervention in Child Sexual Abuse. Lexington Books, 1982

Discovery

How can you describe such a thing? It's too horrible, too shameful to be true. "I have to tell you something. It's true. I had a sexual relationship with her." We are driving the long miles home from the hospital. It is almost dark. I can see the lights of town in the distance, and I wonder if everyone with a light on knows about this and will desert me because of it. I feel this huge hard lump in my chest. My heart hurts so much. I wonder if it will stop and end the pain so I won't have to go on. There are so many tears. None of them can get out. Besides, I'm so angry just then that I'd like to grab the wheel and throw the car in the ditch. Anything but death is too good for the monster beside me. "I'd kill you both if I could!" That's all I can say. No other words will come. There are more of them. Then there are tears, and they can't get out either. I will explode soon. It will all be over, no more pain, no more shame, no more lying. Pretending, hoping, praying for no more craziness, just blissful peace.

How could he? He knew it was wrong. He did it before and lost his family. Now he has done it again. Where will it end??? How could he care so little for us? How horribly selfish can one person be? No wonder he got the damn hepatitis! Of course.

Of course! Oh, my God, they knew. They knew. The nurses and doctors, even the ones at work—they knew he got it from her. They knew and didn't care enough to help me. They knew and they thought I knew and they judged me. They thought I knew and that I didn't mind. How can I live with the shame? How can I face them? How can I ever tell them I did not know?

Now that I think back, I did know there was something wrong, I did. I remember that day coming back to the house, finding the doors locked. (We had just been out painting the house not ten minutes ago. Where are they? Why didn't they finish the job?) My key didn't work. (It's locked from the inside!) He answers the door, stuffing his shirt in his pants. "I was resting."

"I forgot the Tide."

(Why did he lock the door? It's dangerous here. Danger!! Get out of here. Get the Tide and leave! Where is his daughter? Is she all right?) In her bunk. Calling her name, "Are you okay?" Silence. Stillness. No response. (Okay! Okay! If that's how you want it, okay!) As I leave the house, he holds me tight, kisses me, and whispers, "I love you." (What does he mean? The door was locked!)

I'm on the road now thinking about that scene. For an instant in my brain, there is the idea: "They are lovers. It's true." In the next instant is the idea: "That's okay. If I really am pregnant, I'll at least have a baby. I can raise it all by myself. I don't need him, never really did. I'll just ignore him. I'll get my own place and let them rot."

I argue with myself: "How can I be so distrusting? Just because he did it fifteen years ago. He's had treatment, lots of it. How can I be so mean-minded? She has had a terrible time, the drugs, the prostitution, the rejection by her parents. She just needs love, real love, and she'll be all right. Where is my Christian behavior now? Isn't this one of those times I am supposed to forgive and turn the other cheek?" OH, GOD. How can I go on? How did I get in this mess? How do I get out? Forget it. It's too much. I am crazy. I must stop tormenting myself with these awful ideas! Pray that I am pregnant so then I can have a baby and do it right.

Turning into the lane, I'm brought back to reality. I have to get into bed with this person who just told me he did, in fact, have an incestuous relationship with his teenage daughter. Crawling, shivering sensation all over my skin. The dirt will rub off on me. Then I remember: I have been sleeping with this man for almost a month since she called the cops on him.

It's too late. I am already contaminated, and too full of shame to care if I get any dirtier. Besides, it's my bed, my house. I pay all the bills, and I am going to sleep. Why shouldn't I? I didn't do anything wrong. He hasn't really touched the real me, the good person inside of me. I never let anyone in there, so it's not contaminated and never will be.

I'm too tired to care or do anything about these feelings. I can barely get out of the car and into the house. I can barely get my clothes off. Any movement is such a strain, I am exhausted. (Maybe God will take me tonight so I won't have to wake up in the morning.)

❊ ❊ ❊

Looking back after four years of couples and personal therapy, I am beginning to see what it was I did, and did not know how to do, that led to my ending up in that situation.

The story, at least my part of it, started when I was growing up. There are certain things that I learned then that made it easy for me to be attracted to my husband, and, eventually, to be unsuccessful in my relationship with him and my step-daughter. Now I know that I can learn new ways of dealing with the most important people in my life, and be more likely to have success in my relationships. The better I become in this endeavor, the more likely my step-daughter is to see that there is hope. It is possible to get help, to get better, and to break the cycle of incestuous abuse. That's the point of this writing. There is a need in me to reach out and do what I can to help someone else discover that there is a way, a healthy, happy way to break the incest cycle.

"Don't let your anger show, ever." That is one of the things I learned as a young child that has caused me pain. When I learned not to show my anger, I also learned that somehow I wasn't worthy of having and displaying feelings, especially anger, sadness and pain. So I put all those feelings away, deep inside, convinced that I was somehow lacking. How I envied those who could say what they felt! They were whole people. How I hoped that I would be one someday, too!

I tried so hard to follow all the rules and be a good girl. I never disobeyed. As time went by, the strain became too much. I became sickly with chronic problems that kept everyone from noticing that I wasn't perfect anymore. But I knew. I stuffed the guilt back inside, and got sicker.

On the outside, I was everyone's idea of a good child. I did well at school, had talent as an artist, took piano lessons, sang, joined Girl Scouts, church school, volunteer work at the hospital, and generally met everyone's expectations but my own. By the time I met my husband, I had been widowed and was still not grieving. I stuffed those feelings, too.

When he confided in me the truth about his first assault on his other daughter, I felt revulsion. Then it turned into something else. I realized that he was much less perfect than me, so maybe I wasn't the worthless person I thought I was. I began to feel superior. I stuffed the feelings of pain and revulsion, as usual. That allowed me to continue exploring the relationship.

Later when she came and things started to feel wrong—the way she looked at me when I came in the room and found her sitting on his lap; the time he flew into a violent rage and ordered me out of my house because I served the corn on the cob wrong to her—I stuffed the feelings. I'll never know what would have happened if I could have said how I felt. That's part of the legacy of incest that I pray my granddaughter or her husband will never know.

I did get mad enough one night to challenge his behavior and hers. He jumped out of bed, hit me, and told me to get out! But it was my house. I was the only one working. I paid all the bills and he was telling me to leave if I didn't like it! I didn't leave, mostly because I still believed that if I couldn't show my feelings, I must not be worth very much. I probably deserved this since I couldn't be perfect. I did nothing. The situation got worse. I stuffed my feelings.

Earlier in our relationship, he and I produced a baby. Something was wrong, though. The tests showed the baby was not healthy and neither was I. I was too old. True to form, I decided that I couldn't handle both a baby and the man I took care of as if he were a baby. The final result was an abortion that tore my heart out. I stuffed the feelings, all of them.

Shortly after that, he got a job, met another woman, and began to have an affair. I knew there was something really wrong, but I stuffed my feelings and carried on. I was withdrawing and becoming less and less able to tell right from wrong. It was difficult to make any value judgments where my well-being was concerned. Finally in a drunken outburst of guilt, he told all about it. I stuffed my feelings, tried to be the "perfect wife" and "live with it." I said nothing and went on as if it never happened. But I'm not perfect, so the resentment, the hurt, and the awful, overwhelming anger crept out of me. I never let him forget how wounded I had been.

I couldn't help either of them avoid the relationship. They were filling the feeling void I created by not being able to care for myself. But then, if I could have valued myself and expressed my feelings all my life, I would never have stayed in the relationship to begin with.

So now we work together to break the cycle. It's hard work, but nothing will ever hurt me as much as that night of discovery.

Robot

"Ms. Morris, this is Roni, Jane's roommate. She's taken an overdose of pills and alcohol."

Inside, I was screaming, "God, will it ever end?" Outwardly, I sounded calm. "What is her condition? Where is she?" All through the long night and the next two days while my daughter was in intensive care, I did all the right things. I gave her support. I helped my youngest, Sandra, with her feelings. I was the information center for the rest of the family and others who cared about Jane.

No, it is not over yet, but it is different. Because even though I do the "right things" for everyone else, I also do what is right for me. I called on my support system. I cried and asked for the support I needed. I felt, I understood what I felt, and I was not alone. It will never be all over. The residuals of sexual abuse will always be part of me, but I am a different person than I was almost five years ago.

I have always loved holidays and one of my favorites was the 4th of July. No worries about the right presents or fancy meals. Even at 34, I still ooh'ed and ah'ed at fireworks. This 4th of July, my daughters and I were visiting my parents. My mom had made potato salad. Dad was cooking his famous barbecue. The sun was warm and I was feeling relaxed. But I could tell something was wrong with Jane, my fourteen-year-old. When we finally had some time alone, I asked her what was wrong.

"Mom, I'm not imagining it. Brad—" (her stepfather) "—is touching me sexually. I can't handle it any longer," I knew in my heart that she was right and it had to stop.

Two years earlier when she was only eleven, she had told me, "Daddy tickles me in private places." I confronted Brad with this. He denied it. I was so confused and frightened. I discussed it with my best friend. She said I put the idea in Jane's mind because I was so worried about the girls ever being abused. As usual, I accepted the responsibility. If Brad was doing something wrong, surely this would frighten him enough to stop him.

This was my third marriage. I loved Brad and I had no idea what else to do.

But now it was two years later. Somehow I knew Jane was right. I had to do what was right for her. Our life was going to be very different.

The next morning, I called my friend Linda to ask her advice. She had been the human resource aid at our church for the last two years, so I hoped she would have some idea about what I should do. She told me to call the crisis line and report the abuse. So I called a complete stranger in a strange town. I told her my husband was sexually abusing my daughter. I thought it was the hardest action I would ever have to take, but it was only the beginning.

Within an hour, a case worker was at my parents' house. She explained to me that we would have to return to Seattle to file charges because the crime was committed there and would have to be prosecuted where committed. "Crime," "prosecuted," "charges"—these words tore at me. She then explained she would have to take Jane's statement without my being present, and that the children would not be allowed to live with Brad again. Suddenly, I was afraid I would lose my girls. She reassured me that if I did what was correct for the girls, I wouldn't lose them.

While she took Jane's statement, I began making calls to Seattle. I talked to our new case worker in Seattle, discussed how we would confront my husband, and arranged for Jane to stay with a friend so she would be safe while we were in Seattle.

So I started to end eight years of my life. Brad and I had dated for two years before we were married, and we had been married for six years. I loved this man, yet my children must come first. It was not just a husband but a home I was losing.

I had never had roots before I was 26. My father was in the military. We moved an average of every nine months. Both of my parents were estranged from their families, so I had little family connection. When I met Brad, I had two children: Jane, seven, and Sandra, two. Brad gave me things I had never had before. Washington had been his home all his life. He had lots of relatives and his own home. His home was a sailboat, but it was his, and it became mine.

Seattle became my home. I invested all I had in being a part of that city. For the first time in my life, I had close friends. I learned I could have an impact in areas that I cared about. At the time charges were brought against Brad, I led one of the first inner-city chapters of 4-H. We had even received a grant from Chevron Oil for the project we developed and carried out for beautifying a portion of the inner city. I had been directing a soup kitchen for four years. I had formed relationships with many of the street people, low income residents, and southeast Asian refugees. I had just finished three weeks worth of work getting fifteen inner-city children registered for church camp.

This work was part of my identity. I loved the work and I loved the people. I worked hard to give dignity to everyone I worked with. I was part of a loving church and I felt I belonged. But if my daughters and I stayed in Seattle now, we would have to live in poverty and fear. My health had deteriorated to the point I could only work half-time. On that salary, I couldn't provide a home for the girls that wasn't in a poverty area. I worked in those places. I couldn't do that to the girls. I knew Brad wouldn't leave us alone. So I had to leave so much I cared about. But first I had to face Brad.

I called Brad to tell him we would be home on Tuesday. We were actually returning on Monday, but I lied because the authorities were going to meet us so they could interview Jane and keep her from Brad. But I made a mistake when I gave Brad the date. When Jane and I stepped off the train, he was standing there. I shielded Jane and told him to wait there. I found Jane's caseworker, left Jane with her and walked back to him.

If I had any doubts about Jane's story, the look on his face would have been enough to convince me of the truth. He was very frightened and asked me what was happening. All I could say was I would meet him at the boat later that day and would explain. I turned and walked away. I felt every fiber in my body scream, but I walked on and did what I had to. I filed charges against my husband.

During the next few hours, I sat alone as first the case worker, then the prosecuting attorney, and finally the police took Jane's statements. They had to talk to her alone so there was no chance my presence would affect her statement. I know these interviews couldn't have been any longer than 45 minutes each, but they felt hours long.

I remember during one of them, I was sitting on a narrow wood bench. The walls and floor of the hallway were of green marble. I felt so cold and alone. None of the people passing me even seemed to notice I was there. I felt frozen to the bone.

Then they gave me the statements to read. I felt so much sadness. It was like reading a story of torture in a concentration camp. "My poor little girl! My poor little girl!" I screamed these words in my heart. I would do whatever was necessary for her safety and healing. I felt guilt because I had not protected her.

Then they explained to me what would happen to Brad. He would be arrested and charged with sexual abuse. If he plead guilty, he would be given a deferred sentence and probation, provided that he was accepted in a therapy program for sexual abusers. If he pleaded innocent and was found guilty, he would be sentenced to prison.

Now it was time to face Brad. Our caseworker explained that she could talk to Brad, but I chose to tell him. He was my husband. Once again, I had the sense of having no option. I had to do what was right for my children and my husband. I had to stand strong, keep on moving. I thought to myself, "Don't let go. They need you. Just keep that pain flowing through. Don't stop for even a minute. Keep calm. Take care of them all. You have no choice. This is your life and it will always be hard. Hold tight. You know how to be rigid to hold it all in. They need you."

As I entered the boat, I saw Brad sitting with his head bent. I began telling him about the events of the past few days, Jane's statements, and my actions. I explained what the authorities said, and what actions they would take. Then I explained that I believed Jane. I made it very clear that if Brad forced Jane to testify in court that I would have nothing else to do with him. I assured him if he cooperated and got help, that I would support him and continue as his wife. He began to weep. He wept for the next three days. It almost broke me. I came close to yelling, ''Stop! Please stop!'' but I just went on.

The next three days, I closed down most of my life. I found another bookkeeper to handle my accounts. I resigned my volunteer positions and presented proposals for transition for all of them. I packed the girls' belongings and said many good-byes. I consoled Brad and spent time with Jane to help her. I resigned myself to live for Brad and the girls.

I realize now I felt I had no right to all the things and people I loved. Many people around me said I was using great inner strength, but it felt more like shackles to me.

The first few weeks in Montana, we lived with my parents. My father was upset with me because I brought outsiders into a ''family'' situation, and because I left Brad. Mom was furious because I was supporting Brad. It would be years before I understood the depth of her reaction.

Sandra, my ten-year-old, felt confused and left out. I had made the mistake of not telling her right away what had happened. She could tell that things were wrong, but she had no information. That left her feeling scared and lost. She and Brad were still in contact. She felt torn between Jane and Brad.

Jane was beginning the process of releasing years of pain, anger, fear and confusion. She was in individual therapy weekly and would soon begin in group therapy with other sexually abused girls her age. I read everything I could get my hands on, asked questions of the therapists, and was always on alert. I would help Jane get well. I would not let anything happen to her again. I stopped taking my medicine because much of her abuse had happened at night when I was in a deep sleep due to my medicine. I would not allow myself to relax and put her in danger again.

Meanwhile, I was also deeply involved in Brad's therapy. I spent hours on the phone with him after the girls were in bed so it would not upset them that I was on the phone with him. The sense of being a robot continued—a machine functioning for everyone else, but feeling nothing—except doomed.

About one month after we returned to Montana, the depth of Jane's pain was expressed on a night of agony. I heard her cry out during the night. I went into her room. She was on the floor. I gathered her into my arms. She began to weep, a deep bone-chilling crying, a hysterical crying out. Little of her words were understandable except for the phrase, ''Mommy, it was so horrible,'' which she repeated over and over. I held her and rocked her for a long time. My mother came in and tried to get me to quiet her because, she said, of the others in the house. Somehow I knew Jane needed to cry until she was ready to stop on her own. So I continued to rock her and speak gently to her. I prayed over and over, "Please God, don't let me lose her. Keep her safe."

I don't know how long she wept, but she finally cried herself to exhaustion. I laid her in her bed and covered her up. The only time I had allowed myself to cry since the 4th of July was on the trip back to Seattle. I listened to Barbra Streisand love songs and allowed quiet, slow tears to run down my cheeks when no one could see me. Yet I understood Jane's need to weep.

This wasn't the only contradiction inside of me at this time. I felt doomed and sentenced to pay for my badness, yet I also knew God loved and cared for me. Serving Him is very important to me. Thankfully I found a church of my denomination when I returned to Montana, and they opened their arms to me. The girls and I had nothing but our clothes, no furniture, no household goods. We were starting all over from scratch, but God and the members of my church met all our needs. I mentioned one Sunday that I was saving store coupons to get dishes. By the next Sunday, the church had collected enough coupons for me to get a full set of dishes. I became involved in the life of the church as Sunday school superintendent, children's choir director, Sunday school teacher, and anything else the church needed. But I put a wall around my insides. I couldn't stand the idea of losing friends again.

I got a job, rented a house for the girls and I, and settled down. But being involved in Jane's therapy began stirring memories, feelings of pain inside me. During one of our joint sessions, Jane said to me, "I know you don't understand what I went through." I interrupted, "Yes, I do understand. My father sexually abused me." Jane and her therapist looked at me with surprise. "It wasn't as bad as your abuse, but I was abused."

But it was Jane's session, and after all, my abuse happened a long time ago. Although I knew Jane's abuse wasn't her fault, I felt responsible for my own. I didn't feel it was necessary for me to deal with my victimization. Jane and her therapist didn't seem to feel that it was important either. The only other person I had ever told was Brad. I told him how horrible it was for me, and how I never wanted it to happen to my children. He abused Jane anyway. Sharing that part of me just caused my pain. I felt like I must be bad. People didn't react with caring when I told them.

Soon after this, Jane's therapist told me about a support group for wives of sexual abusers. At first, I was resistant about joining this group. The only other experience I had with support groups, I ended up being the caretaker of everyone else. I didn't need any more people to be responsible for now. But I met with the therapists that would lead the group. I liked them right away. Deep inside my robot, I felt a deep longing for something, anything just for me.

The first night we met, the therapists told us it would take a while for trust to develop among the members of the group. We started by listing the emotions we felt when we learned about the abuse. Words flowed out of us and onto large sheets of paper—confusion, fear, anger, disbelief, guilt, dirty, ostracized, doomed. We quickly became a unit. I could sense the surprise that the therapists felt at how quickly the group formed. But I also felt the hunger in the other wives. We met after group to have coffee and talked for hours. This was a turning point for me.

Many issues were dealt with during the next years. Day in, day out, we dealt with our children, our husbands and ourselves. We consoled each other, confronted each other, and taught each other.

Two very important issues were confronted by me during this time. The first was the relationship with my father. Part of the involvement in the healing of our children required us to learn about the process of incest. The more I learned, the more I remembered, and the more I became aware of the terror I lived in.

When I was 17, my father came home from Vietnam. One night when he was drunk, he came into my bedroom. For years I had been afraid of this. It had always seemed wrong the way my father looked at me and talked to me. I felt it was bad, and that something bad would happen between us. All I can remember of that night is fear, so deep that my body and soul froze. Everything turned black, deep ebony black.

Soon after that, my family and I moved again. They went to Europe and I went to a college in the States. Even though I had been an honors student in high school, I couldn't handle college. I felt I was crazy, and I couldn't function. I had no way of knowing that I was suffering trauma from the sexual abuse from my father, high school teachers, and my boyfriend. All I felt was crazy and filthy.

I dropped out of school, which made my father furious, and went to join my boyfriend, Ron. Soon I was pregnant, very sick, and deserted by Ron. I wrote my family to tell them how sick I was and to ask if I could come home. They had always told me they would be there for me, but the letter I received back told me it would be too embarrassing to have me come home. The doctors told me I might die, but all my parents cared about was their position in society.

So I went on welfare. Ron showed up again when I was seven months pregnant and asked me to marry him. I did. He became heavily involved with drugs. He was physically and mentally abusive to me. When our first child, Jane, was eight months old, I miscarried our second baby. I weighed 92 pounds, was very ill and desperate. I called my parents to ask for help. I guess because there was Jane to care about this time, they brought me home. I was beaten physically and spiritually. At 19, I already felt 85 years old.

One day as I was cutting vegetables for salad, my father asked me if I liked oral sex. He then explained that Mom didn't like it, but he did. He said if we had oral sex it wouldn't be wrong because it wasn't intercourse. I felt like I was going to vomit. It was all I could do to keep from cutting my fingers off. The desire to cut and hurt myself was overwhelming. All I can remember was fighting the desire to cut off my fingers.

I had to get away. I was worried about how to take care of Jane. I asked Mom if she would keep Jane until I got settled in the States. She said yes, but I would have to sign papers of temporary custody. So I went to the military judge and had papers drawn up. I took them home to my parents. My dad read them and said they weren't good enough. I said, "This is what you asked for." He took hold of the front of my dress and back-handed me. He hit me so hard my dress ripped and I collapsed on the floor.

The next day, I signed papers to give him custody of my daughter. I left soon after that. I didn't get her back until months later. He frequently reminded me that he had custody of Jane and that he could take her away whenever he wanted to.

So I lived in terror for years, during which time my family returned to Montana. Jane was now 14. Part of Jane's healing process involved her confronting her abuser and taking her power over her life back from him. Watching this happen for her and learning to stop being manipulated through my group therapy brought to a high pitch my need to confront my father. I wrote him a letter to tell him what he had done to me and how I now knew he could never take Jane away from me again. He wrote me back a letter telling me I was evil, and he had to do what he had done to show me how evil I was. He said I'd always brought destruction on him and that he never wanted me around him. He was disowning me and never wanted to see me again.

Soon after that, he moved my mother, brother and himself all the way to the east coast. I felt I had lost my family, but some things were much better after that. I wasn't afraid all the time. That Christmas was the first holiday I could remember when I wasn't afraid, wasn't waiting to see who would get mad at who and when the yelling would start. I wasn't even aware of the tension I lived with until it wasn't there. My home was safe and peaceful. Christmas was filled with joy. I didn't have to manufacture an illusion of a fairy tale home. I had a real home, full of love.

The other important relationship I dealt with during these years was with Brad, my husband. My plan was to be involved in his and Jane's therapy. When everyone was well, we would all be together again. The deepest desires of my heart were to follow Christ and be a good wife and mother.

I was in constant contact with him, mainly through long letters and frequent telephone calls. I made four trips to Seattle to be with him and take part in therapy sessions with him.

The first trip was in August of the year we moved to Montana. My brother drove out with me because we were hauling back the girls' and my possessions. Brad hung on me, following me like a puppy. He was so desperate and afraid I would abandon him. His demands exhausted me. Everything revolved around his needs. The only notice of my needs emerged from a desire to tie me to him. He kept declaring how much he cared about me, yet his decisions were all based on his needs. He had never earned more than $4,000 a year all the six years we had been married. Yet when his lawyer told him a judge would want him to have a regular job, he went out and found a job starting out at $17,000 a year. But he gave me no money. As we were dividing up the household items, I was only allowed to take items that wouldn't inconvenience him. I was raising two children on $800 a month and dealing with the many problems caused by the abuse, yet I wasn't to inconvenience him. Inside, I sighed and just carried on.

The second visit was at Christmas. I spent Christmas Eve with my daughters and parents in Montana, then went to Seattle to spend Christmas week with Brad. The girls would be spending that week with their adopted father, Joe (my second husband) in Montana. Once again, I was spreading myself thin to cover everyone else's needs.

Brad told me how one of the men in his offenders' group felt it was wrong for me to leave my children at the holidays. I was furious that this pervert would dare to judge my parenting. I asked Brad how this man knew about my actions. Brad explained that he had to tell his group everything about our relationship, even when and how often we had sex. I was sickened, revolted that my very personal life was discussed by a group of sexual offenders, and that they were passing judgment on me. I felt violated and exposed.

By the end of the week, I was exhausted and very lonely. My church always had a family get-together on New Year's Eve. I called the house where it was to be this year to ask my friend what time it would start. She told me that there would be children there, so Brad couldn't come. I told her I was planning to come alone. She told me I wasn't welcome because it would be awkward for everyone. I was devastated. I had spent many special times with this friend. Now because of what Brad had done, I wasn't welcome. I left the next day to go back to Montana. I had never felt so beaten and without hope on a New Year's Day before.

The third trip was for Easter. Joe had taken the girls to visit his mother, so I had the weekend free. Easter had always been special for me in Seattle. I missed the green and the spring flowers. Montana was so brown and cold. Brad said he had been working hard to learn to care about others.

After our first night together, Brad noticed that my underwear was in tatters. The kids needed so much that I had little money to spend on myself. He offered to take me shopping for some pretty undies. I was so excited that he wanted to take me shopping for something just for me and totally frivolous. The air was warm, the trees blooming, and I was home. We picked out several lacy items.

As we were driving home, Brad told me he had to tell me something. According to his therapist, any time he had a fantasy about a minor he was to tell a responsible adult who knew he was a sex offender. He proceeded to tell me he had had a sexual fantasy about Jane, my daughter, while he was shopping with me. I began to retch. I felt like I had been beaten. A moment that was special between my husband and me became fouled by his perversion. I felt stripped of my femininity and any hope of being loved as a wife.

The next morning, we drove to Olympia to attend a sunrise Easter service. I spent my whole time shifting in the crowd to place myself between Brad and the children present. His probation required him to have no physical contact with children. He was panic-stricken every time a child came near.

After this ordeal, I drove him home and went to my home church for Easter breakfast. For years I had cooked breakfast for 200 people, including church members, neighborhood people and street people. That Easter I slipped in the back door and took a seat in the back. Soon one of the "regulars" from the neighborhood saw me and announced I was there. All of the neighborhood and street people stood up and applauded me. I wept. They had not forgotten me, and they still cared about me. After breakfast, I worshipped in my church among friends. That morning, I knew God was with me, no matter what this life handed me.

That evening I just wanted to distance myself from Brad. I sat and read a book. He sat and just stared at me. After about an hour, I couldn't stand it anymore. I went to bed with him so he would leave me alone. I had always been able to "go away" and become an empty husk when having sex. At least he was satisfied and left me alone after that. He fell asleep quickly, but I laid awake for a long time, feeling dirty and alone.

By the next morning, I knew I had to confront Brad. When I told him what I had done the night before, his response was to ask me why I had played the "prostitute" with him. He had manipulated and pushed me up against a wall. When I used the only way out I knew, and he called me a prostitute.

The last time I visited him, it was to read a letter to him and his therapist. I had spent months working on it. I listed all the incidents and behaviors that made me question his ability to have a healthy mature love for me. I felt I was fighting my way through quicksand while I read that letter out loud. Even while I read it, I held on to the hope that he cared enough about me to do the hard things to show real love for me. But his response to my letter was to chew on small trivials. He couldn't see or understand what he was doing to me.

Finally his therapist stopped him, saying he was proving my letter by his action. His therapist asked me what my plans were now. I told them I would file for divorce. His therapist asked if he could copy my letter to use with Brad in his group. Even the ending of my marriage would be a group event.

Brad followed me downstairs and asked me if this meant we wouldn't have lunch together. I felt like I had strips of flesh hanging from my body. I had asked someone I loved to love me enough to try and be healthy. He had whipped me with his words until I knew he would never really love me, and all he could think about was whether I would have lunch with him. As I left, I wanted to run and run, but I slowly walked away. I reached my room and showered for a long time.

I had prayed to God over and over to make me a good wife. He answered my prayer in a very different way than I had dreamed. I loved Brad enough to refuse to enable his sickness. I called Brad to be accountable for his behavior. The term "tough love" has been used to describe the love used by relatives of alcoholics to refuse to enable alcoholism. I had done the hard things over and over to learn not to enable Brad. Now God gave me a sense of peace about divorcing Brad. I had done all I could. I was the best wife I could be to him. I had given the hard love.

In group, I learned about parenting, dealing with manipulations, and how to deal with my co-dependent behaviors. The women were important to me, but I reached a point where I couldn't stand to do it anymore. I didn't know what was wrong with me. I was becoming very aware that I was a victim of sexual abuse. I wanted the other women to understand me. They were mothers of victims, and they had worked very hard to understand and support their daughters. When I felt they didn't understand me, I acted like I had when I was a youth and ran away so they couldn't hurt me anymore. The feelings I had experienced as an abused child were emerging from inside of me. I didn't know how to tell anyone. So I told everyone I was fine and didn't need therapy, and quit group.

The kids were doing well, including the foster children I had taken into my home. I had been able to buy my own home. My life was going fine, but there was an intensity of feelings building up inside me that I was having a hard time controlling. Whenever they escaped, they blasted at my oldest daughter, Jane. Over the three and a half years since we had left Seattle, I had learned to yell less and less at the kids. Most of the time I was much more relaxed and sensible with them, but these volcanic reactions would erupt on Jane without much notice. I was very afraid she would walk the same life trail I had. I didn't want that to happen.

Then a crisis hit that I couldn't keep contained inside my robot casing. My illness had finally been diagnosed as Reiter's Syndrome, a form of ankylosing spondylitis. My symptoms were increasing. Many days I couldn't even dress by myself. My eyes were attacked, and for a long time, I could not even do my needlework which I loved doing. The pain was very intense. I spent considerable time and energy learning to deal with the pain and my feelings about it. Sandi, my therapist, and I did considerable work on these feelings. Then the disease attacked my lungs, and for months I could barely breathe. Reiter's Syndrome kills by reducing lung capacity until pneumonia settles in and cannot be treated. I had to face the fact that I could be close to death. Facing these emotions, and coming to terms with them brought about many changes in me, one of which was beginning to trust Sandi. I had never trusted anyone else before. But by letting out some of my emotions, I was creating a crack in my emotional dam.

I often felt during that time as if I was swimming for my life. Sometimes I felt like I could float, but I was always afraid I was going to be overwhelmed.

The crest of the flood had hit when Jane and I had a very serious fight and she moved out. I couldn't sleep and even driving in my car was a battle with the voice that told me to drive off the road and end it all. But something inside of me wanted to live, so that little part of me called out to the only person I trusted. "Sandi, I'm in trouble," I whispered.

I don't know how Sandi knew from that sentence how much trouble I was in, but she immediately took action. Soon I was in the support center at St. Peter's Hospital, being tucked into bed by two gentle nurses. I was so tired. It was a relief to be cared for.

The next morning, I awoke knowing that this was a turning point for me. I had lived with deep internal pain for many years. If I didn't find help for that pain, I wasn't sure I would make it much longer. Part of me felt selfish for being here—after all, my kids needed me and I was missing work—but it was time to take care of me.

I spent ten days on the psych unit. Besides beginning the conscious steps toward healing, two major events happened. The first involved meeting Susan. She was the main therapist. The first real contact I had with her was when she took me out of a group session for an individual session. I had been trying to explain to the group about why I was so worried about Jane. I remember saying, "You don't understand how bad it can be . . ."

Susan homed in on the intensity of my fear. When we were in her office, she asked me to continue to explain about how Jane could be hurt by men. As I began to talk, she touched my shoulder. I began to shake uncontrollably. As I tried to stop, Susan told me to continue, that I was releasing terror, and I needed to let it go. As I continued to shake, she held me and I wept until I was exhausted.

Then as I rocked in a big wooden rocker and held a Raggedy Ann doll, she began to ask me questions. Then she explained to me that my behavior and thoughts were not crazy, but normal for a person who had been abused. There was even a name for my symptoms, post traumatic stress disorder, the same problem some of the Vietnam veterans were suffering from. She understood so much, and she shared considerable information with me. I began to trust her. She also explained that she thought my abuse wasn't restricted to the two incidents I remembered because of the many different symptoms I had.

She helped me to begin to center on healing my own life. Even after I left the hospital, Susan would continue to be a part of my healing. She leads a support group for adult survivors of abuse. I would do intense and important work for healing myself as a member of that group.

The other crucial event while I was in the hospital was a session with a doctor during which he challenged me to stop hating myself and forgive myself. I had always felt I was very evil inside, and that all the bad things that had happened to me were my own fault. Every mistake I made, I drove another nail into my heart to punish myself. I felt doomed to continue having this much pain. He brought me to the point where I knew that I had to fight the battle with myself or I was never going to be safe or without the feeling of being two people in one body: The "outside person" and the person I had hid inside. I was always afraid that people would learn who I really was, and then either reject me out of revulsion or hurt me. But this gentle man stood there and told me he felt compassion for me and that I had a right to self-love and existence. He touched a deep longing in me. I can only explain it as a desire to connect with other people and be loved.

So began a very intense time for me. I had to make a choice to center on myself, and that was the complete opposite of how I had functioned and survived for 37 years. I also had to choose to walk into my memories and deal with them.

For months, I battled within myself, during the therapy sessions with Sandi, and in group sessions. I agonized through the nights and even yelled at God. I finally told Him I could not resolve the conflict between the need to be "selfish" to heal myself and being selfless to follow Him. If I was wrong to center on myself, He would have to let me know. I couldn't stand this turmoil anymore. I needed to try and heal. He answered me with the verse, "Love your neighbor as yourself." He also sent me a loving member of my church who listened, prayed with me, and encouraged me to do what I must do to heal. She even prayed me into bed and to sleep when nightmares would terrorize me.

Finally one night I had the courage to expose to my group the fact I felt evil inside, and ask them if any of them felt that way. My therapists, Sandi and Susan, and all the material I read, told me that abuse victims always feel at fault and evil, but that they aren't at fault or bad. I could believe that about the children I worked with, but I couldn't believe it about myself. When I asked the women in my group, there were sixteen women there. As I explained how I felt inside, the room was filled with women reacting with tears or nods. Each of us had the same feeling. I knew these women. I knew they weren't bad or evil. I cared for them. I wept and wept. Maybe I wasn't evil. Maybe I was valuable in myself.

That night greatly increased my trust in Sandi's and Susan's work. I threw myself into the healing even harder. I began to look at fragments of memories.

I had had a recurring nightmare since I was very young. In the nightmare, I was about three years old, sitting on a tricycle, and looking up with a big smile. Suddenly a man was standing over me. Then he hit me so hard I fell off the bike. Every time I went back to that memory, I had a sense that my grandfather was involved. So I called my mother to ask her what my grandfather looked like. I didn't remember even knowing him and I had never seen a picture of him. I knew my mother was estranged from him.

She considered her stepfather her "real" father. She asked me why I wanted to know. I explained about my dream. She seemed irritated with me, but gave me a vague description of him.

A couple of days later, my mother called me back. She began to tell me about my grandfather's kidnapping me when I was three years old. When she got me back, my legs were black and blue. My grandfather said I had been bad and wet my pants a lot, so he had to discipline me. Feelings and memories flooded over me like huge waves breaking on a beach. I would recover many other memories. In all, the count of my abusers came to eight men and three females. It started when I was three years old and continued until I was thirty. I had been beaten, raped, and even left to die, yet I had survived.

Digging through these memories also brought the feelings back to me. Fear, terror, abandonment, shame, numbness—all these I experienced, but the emotion I avoided the most was anger. I was so afraid of anger. Anger always hurt other people. I was full of rage and terrified I would hurt Sandi or someone else if I released it. I battled releasing my anger, not realizing I was already using anger in a positive way. I had started to fight back. I was speaking out about sexual abuse. The more I spoke, the more people opened up to me about what had happened to them. I became a public speaker. I spoke to groups as varied as church groups, girls' schools, and all 200 employees of the local telephone company. I was involved in the healing of many abuse victims. I was using my anger for good. I also discovered that that anger was what had helped me survive for years.

Although Sandi helped me realize I was using my anger to help others, I was still frightened and ashamed of it. But that anger became very precious to me because of an interaction I had with prisoners convicted of sexual crimes.

Their therapist was having difficulty helping them learn empathy, and felt that if people who had been hurt by abuse shared what it was like, these men would be able to understand better. I had no sympathy for these men, but if I could help protect another person from being hurt by them, I was willing to go. One of the women who had been in the support group for wives of abusers went also. Sandi and another woman therapist went with us.

As I walked through the prison doors and heard them slam behind me, I felt the fear and anger building in me. We were led into a meeting room. I placed myself so I could see Sandi and Jody, the woman from my former support group. Soon, twelve men entered and sat in the circle. They introduced themselves by giving their first name, the crime they were convicted of, and the victim of their crime. It was like being in a room with all of the people who offended against me. Fathers and grandfathers who had committed incest, rapists, even a teacher who had abused a student, all were there.

Jody and I began telling what it had been like having our children abused, what it did to them and to us. Then one of the men began to talk about his guilt about his daughter and her child which had been conceived because of his incest. Rage boiled out of me and I yelled at them. I had carried five babies in my body, and they had all died because my body was so torn up inside. Doctors kept saying to me, "Why is your body so torn up?" My babies had died because I had been abused.

And I had lost so much more. I was an honor student, yet hadn't been able to deal with college. I had lived with shame and constant fear, and much of my talent was locked inside me. I talked about how they had taught me to lie because I was afraid, how my sexuality was my shame, and how I hated my own body.

For three hours, Jody and I shared with these men and they shared with us. As those men really listened to me and heard me, as some of them cared for me, I experienced a deep healing. I had been heard and grieved for.

Then I felt another connection with these men, compassion for them. I was able to see their pain. They were damaged, too. I will never excuse their actions—there is never an excuse for abusing others—but I was able to see the pain and the loneliness in those men. My anger led me to a place where I could find healing and forgiveness for those who had hurt me, and it keeps me going to continue to fight abuse.

I have continued to work on my healing, and I am actively involved in helping others to heal. My oldest daughter and I have reconciled. She is doing well in college and continues her recovery. My youngest daughter has grown into a healthy teenager. I am renewing a relationship with my parents. My mother shared with me that she was sexually abused as a child. That helps me to understand a lot of what has and has not happened between us. I have gone back to college to earn my degree in psychology and become a counselor. I earned straight A's my first year back. But the most important achievement is that I like who I am, and I'm glad to be who I am.

Many people have been a part of my healing, and I am very appreciative of all of them. But Sandi had a very special part. Her compassion, in addition to her professional excellence, has been a great gift to me, and I am very thankful.

I recently attended a spiritual healing conference. During a mass for healing, I felt the need to ask for healing of the hatred I have had for my body. The woman who prayed for me told me she had been given the following words for me. "Jesus sees you as his queen. He has placed a white, royal robe about your shoulders, and a crown upon your head. Walk with dignity and pride." Some days that robe feels like satin and flows back from me as I stride along. Other days it feels like a white fur that I wrap around myself to protect myself from the cold outside. I wear it with pride. I have value.

Inside I Was Screaming

I will start at the beginning. For me, that's the night Kristy, my teenage daughter, told me that her brother, Nick, had sexually molested her. Nick no longer lived in our home. I guess she finally felt safe enough to disclose the abuse. I am still not sure if I can put into words how I felt. That pain is hard to describe. I know I went into shock. I felt numb for a while, but not long enough. I talked to Kristy very calmly, and I kept reassuring her of how much I loved her. I told her everything would be all right. Inside I was screaming. I wanted to be alone. I wanted to cry. I wanted to believe her, but it just would not register that this was a reality.

As soon as Kristy went to bed, I called the emergency line at the mental health center to talk to someone, and to try to regain some of my sanity. I talked for hours. I was asked if I had hit Kristy or called her a liar. I had not. I did not call anyone in my family that night. I don't know why. I must have spent a week or more in total confusion. I managed to go to work for a few days. I did things at work and at home without knowing what I was doing. Everything was going so fast. My mind just kept spinning.

Kristy initially disclosed her sexual abuse to her friend's counselor at the mental health center. One thing I managed to do was call him. He told me that the law required him to report the incest to the welfare office. I never even thought that could be an issue. That was the last straw. I had all that I could handle at that time. I was at work when I made the call. I fell apart. I was screaming and crying. I was so scared. The counselor, Tom, told me to come in for a counseling session because I was so upset. He thought I should talk to someone immediately. So I left work in tears, not knowing what would happen next.

Tom arranged for me to meet with a woman who was on call as the emergency therapist. I had just finished telling her why I was there and what happened to my daughter when someone brought Kristy in to us. She had fallen apart at school. Neither of us was coping too well.

The therapist started telling me how sick my son was. "He's sick, sick, sick, sick, I tell you. He's perverted. He needs to be turned over to the authorities." She was hitting the table with her fist as she told me this. I understood that her feeling about sexual abuse was very strong. I was still pretty upset when I left. Neither of us said very much. We just cried a lot.

I met this same therapist about a week later. She came over to where I was sitting, and apologized to me for having broken down that day because she was under so much stress. I hadn't even realized she was stressed out.

Quite often, I wanted to get into my car and drive away as far as I could go, just me. Then I would think, "No, I can't leave Kristy. She needs me now more than ever." Then I'd think of my other son, John. "Well, I will take John with us. I can't leave him either." These feelings were very strong, but reality always sank in. I knew this was not possible. I had to stay home and work. I had to face this.

I finally decided that the best thing to do at this time would be for me to take a week's vacation. This way I could pull myself together, and I could spend a lot of time with Kristy. She was frequently ill and vomiting, and refusing to attend school. I was worried. Most of the time we just sat together and did not talk a lot. I did keep telling her how much I loved her, and how sorry I was that such a horrible thing had happened to her. I tried to reassure her that everything would be all right, even though I was not sure everything would be all right.

I was very frightened about how to deal with this crisis. This was something I knew nothing about. This was not a drug or alcohol problem. My family was used to dealing with that. Sometimes I wished the problem was alcohol or drugs. Then I would at least know what to do.

Our next step was to join the support group at mental health. Kristy went on Tuesday afternoons after school with six other girls who had been sexually abused. I went to the women's group for mothers of sexually abused children Thursday nights for two hours. I don't think I would have made it if it hadn't been for this group. I have always been a very shy and quiet person, so it was very hard for me to walk into a room full of strange women who knew I was there because of sexual abuse in my family. At first I felt a lot of shame, and I felt responsible for what had happened.

It was hard at first, very hard. The first few times I went, all I could do was cry. I cried for myself. I cried for my daughter. I cried for the women in that room and for their children. I was in pain. I hurt real bad. I wanted to take all of my daughter's pain and put it inside of me so she wouldn't hurt anymore. Then it could all be erased. I was very depressed. I thought I'd never laugh or be happy again in my whole life.

I kept going back to my group because I felt safe there. I could cry freely. I was not alone. We all shared the same pain and grief. I found this very comforting. No one on the outside needed to know the true horror or the details of what had happened. No family members needed to know, only my friends in that room. I could say anything in there and feel good about it. It could be anything about my children or my childhood.

I kept thinking about the parts of Kristy that had been taken away from her, as though Nick had killed some things inside of her. He certainly took away parts of her childhood. He replaced her carefree, happy innocence from her with fear, pain, and punishment, mentally and physically. He often told her she was a bad girl and he had to punish her. Then he would beat her up.

There is not much of her childhood she can remember now, and she is only sixteen. Sibling incest is traumatic. I had not protected her from any of this. That was and is hard for me to deal with. I kept wishing I would have pursued my hunches and figured it out sooner.

I was very angry at my son. I felt that the other women in the group at least had a choice. I did not. They could choose to divorce or stay with their husbands. I could not divorce my son. He was my flesh and blood. I gave birth to him. I raised him. I remember saying again and again, "I want to go back and do it over. I want to do it right this time. Please let me do it over." A lot of feeling, but no reality. Reality was very far away from me at that time. It took me a long time to absorb all the pain and the shock, and to sort out and deal with all of my feelings, and to put my—our—lives back together. It's a long, hard road.

Dealing with Nick at any time has been the most difficult of all. It took several months to even confront Nick. At first, I just wasn't ready to deal with him because Kristy needed so much time and energy. It took all I had to deal with her. Also I feared he would be suicidal or even violent when he learned that I knew. I did not know how he would respond to that information.

Nick would phone me at home. Sometimes I wouldn't talk to him and other times I could. If he called and Kristy answered, she would start vomiting again. She was terrified of him. Sometimes I would drive up to the house with Kristy and see Nick's car there, and we would drive around until he was gone. We were both terrified of him.

It was two months after I learned about Kristy's sexual abuse. No one had confronted Nick about sexually molesting her. I still could not make the decision to press charges against my son, when some unexpected and shocking events took place.

Nick turned eighteen in December. Kristy revealed her story in February. Nick was charged with statutory rape in April. His victim's name was Ann. Because those charges were brought against him, I never had to make that horrifying decision. I thank God for that.

It must have been about June when the authorities confronted Nick with his molestation of Kristy. They told me they had confronted him. Nick called me that day at work and asked me if I could give him a ride to his friend's house where he was staying. I said sure. I thought to myself all day, "He's going to deny it. I know he is." Was I surprised. During the entire ride he made casual small talk.

Finally as he was getting out of the car, I yelled, "Nick, did the Sheriff talk to you today about Kristy?" "Yes, he did." That was it. I couldn't believe it. No explanation, no "I'm sorry," no nothing. That left me feeling empty, with no answers. I knew then that it would be a long time before Nick and I would have any kind of a relationship again. I was right. I needed to hear that he was sorry from the bottom of his heart. It took a long time for that to happen. I did not see or talk to Nick for about five months. He stayed in school, but he did not go to his sex offenders therapy group. I had to quit supporting him financially, as I was having great financial difficulty myself.

I worried about him a lot. I felt as though I had probably lost him forever. I hated the feeling that I had to choose between my children. That's a sad, sad feeling that no mother ever wants to feel.

I felt that Nick had betrayed me. It seemed that every time Nick said, "I love you, Mom," it was a lie. Every time I trusted him or believed in him, he deceived me. His whole life was a lie.

Later Nick told me that was the worst time in his life. He was using drugs and alcohol heavily. To not have a mother to talk to or a family to turn to was unbearable. It was the loneliest time of his entire life.

Nick did confide in me once several years earlier that he had been molested by his cousin. I gave him a totally stupid answer. I told him I was sure that because he was a boy it wasn't traumatic. That was a good one, Mom.

I also had to deal with the impact of the sexual abuse on myself. During the first few months that I was aware of the incest between my children, I found it increasingly difficult to have sex with my husband. I would either burst into tears or I would not want sex at all. At times I would even get sick to my stomach. I began to understand some of Kristy's feelings.

My husband was very understanding. It seems strange how much closer we actually became. I was sure when I told him about Kristy and Nick that he would simply get up, leave, and never come back, but he didn't.

I don't think I really understood at the beginning what kind of horrible ordeal Kristy had been put through.

Reflections Into the Past

Now a lot of past feelings, events, and unanswered questions came to light like magic. Now I can see many signs of Kristy's sexual abuse.

The first incident I remember was second grade. Kristy came running to me one day, "Mommy, kiss me. I love you. I'm a lesbian." Her brothers thought that was so funny. I did not. Of course, I dismissed it right away.

Kristy developed very young. In the second grade, she needed a bra. By the end of the year, she had started her period. She was nine. She would try to hug and kiss her brother at school, which he did not like at all.

The summer she was ten, she babysat for a friend who had a little girl who was about seven. My friend called and said the police had been notified, and had spoken to Kristy. She had been accused of molesting two little boys aged two and four. It was very frightening. I didn't know how to deal with it, so I took Kristy to a psychiatrist. After about four visits, I was assured there was nothing to worry about. It was an isolated incident.

Next we went through a period of time when she seemed infatuated with her brother. How cute he was and how proud she was that he was her brother. I, of course, was very happy that they were so close. There were a few times that I thought it was a little too much, but I dismissed that feeling.

Around this time, Kristy began to change. It was becoming easier to spot changes in her. Nick and Kristy's relationship abruptly changed. Lots of fighting and arguments. He would call her dirty disgusting names such as "whore," "slut," "fat moose," or "fat cow." I would ask him what was wrong with him to even speak to her that way. I would try to make him stop, but without much success. It always made me so angry. I felt powerless.

Kristy would come out of her room to watch TV before going to bed and she would be half naked. I would tell her to put on a robe or something. She would reply, "Why? What difference does it make?" I didn't pick up on that exactly, but I sensed something was going on. I did ask her many, many times if her stepfather had ever touched her or bothered her, and she always said no. It never entered my mind to ask her about her brother. I am almost positive that even with all the clues, a person must be told point blank what has happened. Something inside of me didn't want to put the clues together. It would be too painful. A pain beyond words.

When Kristy was in sixth grade, I was called to the police station. They asked me to bring my two sons with me. The charge was obscene phone calls. As it turned out, the victim was Kristy's ex-boyfriend. It was Kristy who made the calls. Because she had been very ill for a couple of months, the police captain said he would not press charges or speak to her about it, as long as I spoke to her myself. I assured him that it would never happen again.

Kristy

My little Kristy. Oh, how I loved you. My little girl. So tiny, so loving, so cute. She would snuggle right along my neck and make little noises like a whimpering little puppy.

She only weighed five pounds and three ounces at birth. She never seemed to eat enough when she was fed. I had to feed her about every hour. Still she cried a lot. We moved to Great Falls before Kristy was one month old. She started to cry all the time after we moved, so her dad started to spank her before she was a month old.

One night he came home drunk and Kristy was crying. He spanked her and tried to push her crib out the front door. I was able to stop him. I was very lucky because he was so drunk.

The very next day, I called home to Helena for someone to come and get us and move us back. Help was there. As soon as possible, we were back in Helena, but Kristy did not get any better.

One day as I was changing Kristy's diaper, I noticed blood in her stool. I took her to a doctor. He decided to do an exploratory operation on her. She was exactly one month old to the day. I called her dad because I felt he had a right to know. I did not want to go through that ordeal alone. The day before the surgery, I went into Kristy's room and I saw a diaper full of blood. A nurse came in and whisked it out of the room. To this very day, I act as though I never saw it. It was just so scary.

During the operation, all I could think was, "Dear God, am I going to lose my little girl? Please don't take her from me. I love her so much. I could not stand to lose my daughter." Kristy came through the surgery fine except for one thing. She had needle marks on her arm from where they fed her intraveneously. She still has those marks on her today and she hates them.

After the surgery, the doctor said that Kristy had a birth defect. The bowels of her intestine were not connected together. Kristy could not come home right away because she had lost so much weight. She only weighed three and a half pounds at this time, and she needed to weigh five pounds before she could come home.

Things did not get any better. I broke my leg when Kristy was about six months old. I was down in bed completely for about two months. There was no one to care for my children. I had no choice but to put them in foster homes. I cried and cried. I felt as though I was abandoning my children. I was so afraid that the Welfare would not give my children back to me. This fear came from my own childhood. I was taken out of my home when I was fourteen, and I never returned.

In the foster home, things with my other two children, Nick and John, went very well. They were on a ranch, and they loved it. They even rode sheep like rodeo cowboys. But Kristy had asthma, so she could not stay there, and had to be moved to a foster home in town. As soon as I got my walking cast, I went to see my boys. They were doing well. Then I went to see Kristy. At the time of my visit, she was in an asthma crisis. Her lungs were full of mucus and phlegm, and she could not breathe. The foster mother's explanation was, "I do not like Kristy's doctor, and I will not take her to him." So my mother and I rushed Kristy to the doctor. She was put right into the hospital. When she was released from the hospital, Kristy went to another foster home. They were nice people, but the children were separated. Soon all three of my children were returned to me. I was very happy.

Kristy spent a lot of years in school, Head Start, prekindergarten, and kindergarten. Then she did the first grade twice because of reading. At home, Kristy was always there to help out with the cleaning, dishes, or whatever needed to be done.

One summer, I had my sister, who was about twelve or fourteen, babysit for me. I could not afford a regular babysitter. It was that summer that my sister began to sexually abuse Kristy. Kristy was four years old. Nick caught my sister molesting Kristy. Then Nick started his abuse of her. He was nine years old.

First he taught her that this was normal and appropriate for brothers and sisters to be sexual. He groomed her for several years. Grooming means playing and petting each other. She was seven when he had sexual intercourse with her. When she was ten, she started to figure out that it was not right for brothers and sisters to be sexually involved.

For the first few years, their relationship was of love and lovers. Nick acted like her boyfriend. He made her feel special. She believed he loved her. In time that changed. Nick began to use blackmail and threats to obtain sex from his sister:

1. He bribed her with candy or food.
2. He told her, ''Mom won't love you anymore. She will hate you and disown you,'' and ''It will cause Mom lots of pain and be too much for her to handle. It will be all your fault for telling.''
3. He beat her physically with his fists.
4. He put a knife to her throat and threatened to kill her.
5. When she was older, he gave her drugs and alcohol.

Nick sexually abused Kristy in other ways. He made her watch porno movies with him and re-enact the sex acts they had seen. He also would get her drunk or high and then encourage her to have sex with his friends. Many times he would threaten to kill her if she did not do everything he wanted her to do. That must have been so terrifying for her.

When Kristy was twelve, she was finally able to make Nick stop. She had already been deeply hurt. She began to have nightmares. The nightmares were mostly about Nick killing various members of the family, all of the family, or just Kristy. She would be asleep, but awaken me screaming, ''Mommy help me! Mommy help me! Mommy save me!'' She sounded like a five year old. I know now that she was regressing to a little girl again so I could save her from the abuse.

It really hurts me that I did not save her, that I did not protect my daughter. I felt like such a failure. What kind of mother was I to have been so blind and so dumb as to not know what was happening to her in our own home? Oh, Kristy! I am so sorry. I love you so much.

The Illness

Around November when Kristy was in the sixth grade, she became sick. She was vomiting frequently. Of course, I assumed she had the flu. But after two weeks of vomiting every time she ate anything, I took her to the doctor. The doctor ran several tests on her but could find nothing wrong with her. After one month of constant vomiting, the doctor suggested that she go back to school even though she was still ill. We tried that for about a month and a half. But many times the school would send her home anyway. She was getting behind in her school work. She was losing some weight, too.

This was a very hard time for me. I worried constantly about her. I had no idea what was wrong or what to do next. Her appetite remained good. She looked healthy. I became more and more tired and depressed. Finally after what seemed like an eternity, the doctor put Kristy in the hospital. I was so happy. I thought he should have done that a lot sooner than he did. I felt he made her suffer far too long. In the hospital she was put on IV's, and was seen by a psychiatrist named Lois. The vomiting stopped almost immediately. She was checked for anorexia and bulimia. Lois felt Kristy needed to get some feelings out that were inside of her that made her vomit. Lois and the doctor thought it was probably related to school.

We saw Lois five or six times after Kristy was released from the hospital. We went as a group: Nick, Kristy, John and myself. Our meetings centered mainly about our family life. Nick really put up a fight about going, but he went most of the time. We talked about how Nick felt I did not show him enough love, which is something that is very hard for me to do. We also talked about how Kristy felt about school, and what kind of problems she was having at school. It was hard for her to go to school when she would vomit in class. Being teased by boys for having big breasts and being overweight. Her stepfather gave her a hard time at home about her weight also. But never once did Lois or myself pick up one clue to the sexual abuse.

Our second bout of vomiting came when Kristy was in seventh grade, soon after she told me about her abuse. This time I took her to another doctor who was a woman. She seems much more caring and comforting to Kristy, although she also waited three months before she put Kristy in the hospital. This time, they put her in the Support Center (the psychiatric unit). She was there for four days. Then she stopped vomiting on her own. This time we knew Nick was the cause of her psychological illness. At least this time, her counselors knew exactly what they were dealing with. That part made it easier for me. The three months before they put her in the hospital was a very hard time for me.

There was a lot of fear. She had vomited for so many months, I was beginning to think she was never going to be able to quit. I kept thinking about bulimia. I was so scared she might die. I kept that fear at the very back of my mind. I was afraid to even think such a thing.

I could do nothing to make her better or to make her stop vomiting. I just sat and watched day after day. I felt so helpless. I could do nothing to help my own child. Every time she ate anything, it came right back up. She could not keep water down either.

There were many trying times. One morning, she started vomiting as I was driving her to school. I had to pull over to the side of the road and wait for her to finish vomiting. Another time I stood and waited forty-five minutes for her to stop vomiting, and I was late for work. It was a very stressful time for Kristy and myself.

After Kristy came home from the hospital, she improved for a while. She went back to school, and managed to pass seventh grade. Her school counselor kept trying to work with Kristy on her abuse. Kristy did not like her and did not want her help at all. Also at school some of the kids found out about the abuse. They gave her a bad time, teasing her and calling her dirty names. Most of the time she did not even want to go to school. Plus it was very hard for her to concentrate at school. She was stressed and depressed. Her mind was on the abuse issues, not on math and English. She was missing a lot of school. The school started sending me letters saying they were going to take me to court for not making Kristy go to school. I went to her doctor and to her counselor to get letters from them explaining the sexual abuse that Kristy had been through. Then the school set up special hours for Kristy to go to school only in the morning. This helped Kristy get through that year.

Kristy was still under a lot of stress. She was tired all the time. She began having nightmares again and went into a depression. Her doctor decided to put her on anti-depressants. The vomiting stopped for about six months. During this time, we each continued with our group counseling, and tried to deal with our lives and the abuse the best we could. This was also six months without crisis.

The vomiting started again in October of her eighth grade year. This time the pattern was a little different. She started screaming with stomach pain and vomiting. She was screaming so badly that I rushed her to the emergency room at the hospital. They called her doctor. She screamed at least fifteen or twenty minutes until her doctor arrived. She also regressed to a small child. She was screaming, ''Mommy, Mommy, help me!'' over and over again. The combination of the pain, vomiting and regression was very upsetting to me. I kept thinking, ''When is this going to stop? When is it going to be over? How much more can I take?'' Kristy spent a few more days in the hospital on the Support Unit.

When I talked to the doctor, it was clear that it was something psychological that was bothering Kristy. I felt that this must stop at any cost. Kristy, who is very mature and wise for her age, started to talk to her group counselor and to her doctor about going into a foster home. This decision was not made in haste. We both realized it must be done. I would have let her move out of our home forever if that would have made her better. But it hurt deeply, and I cried in group every time I talked about it.

The foster placement was necessary because our home was becoming too much for Kristy. I had taken down every picture of Nick in our house, but everything in her room bothered her and reminded her of Nick.

Kristy did go to live in a foster home in November. We had several meetings with a social worker, who explained the procedure. Kristy could live in a foster home for six months. After that, I would have to go to court and give up my parental rights.

When Kristy moved into her foster home, she changed schools. Things got better right away. She started doing well in school. This seemed to be the positive lift that she needed. In the five months she was there, she became healthy and happy again.

Kristy's placement in a foster home did a lot of good in many ways. The foster parents were a lot more strict than I was, which was good. At this time because of all that Kristy had been through, I was finding it more and more difficult to parent Kristy. Many times, I felt as though I had lost all my parenting skills. After all, I had failed badly when she was younger. I was tired and confused. Kristy also learned that home was not such a bad place after all.

While Kristy was in the foster home, I had the time I needed to rest and to become stronger mentally. It also gave me time to fix up her room. I got her a new bed, new drapes, throw pillows, and a new bedspread. Changing her room made me feel much better. Finally, there was something I could do to make my daughter feel better.

Kristy and her stepfather did not get along well. One positive step I made before Kristy came back home was to tell them both that I would no longer be the middle person between them to try to keep the peace in the family. No more. It was time for them to make a relationship of their own, as friends or as enemies. It was their choice. It was up to them and them alone. Things have been much better between them since. We all seem to be changing for the better. I don't think Kristy will have any more bouts of vomiting.

Nick

Nick, my first born son. A human life entrusted to me to take care of, to love. Something to live for. A meaning for my life.

When Nick was born, his dad went to celebrate. He drank for two weeks.

Nick was born in 1968, his brother John in 1970, and their sister in 1972. I divorced their dad in 1973, and I remarried in 1974. I married their dad's first cousin, which would be their second cousin.

Nick did very well in school. He seemed to attract people. I was pretty poor. I supported my three children by myself. I was a maid in a motel, which does not pay well. When Nick was in second grade, a package came in the mail for him. It was a winter coat. I think his teacher sent it to him, but I'll never know for sure.

In fourth grade when he went to school, he would find gum or quarters with a note saying, "From your anonymous friend." His teacher died of cancer that year. It was very hard for all the kids. Nick also was in the boys choir at the "Y". I was very proud of him.

He was always polite, happy, good natured, and bright. When Nick was seven, he was sexually abused by my cousin who babysat for me sometimes. She was fourteen. When he was eight, he was sexually abused by my sister, who was about twelve years old. She was also abusing Kristy. He then began to groom and molest Kristy.

As he got older, Nick's relationships seemed to be changing with everyone but me. His relationship with his stepfather was getting worse. He and his brother were getting into more fistfights. He remained very loving and caring to me. He made me very proud of him. He was going to be the first person from my family to graduate from high school in almost a hundred years. That was my goal. My children were going to graduate from high school.

When Nick reached his teens, he became more and more uncontrollable and aggressive, even to me. He was continually picking on Kristy and John. He became mean and cruel. He called Kristy a slut and a whore. "You going out to walk the streets tonight, Kristy?" The verbal abuse was terrible. He beat her up, but I never saw that. Now his fights with Kristy make sense to me. I'm sure Nick blamed her for what he did. That way, it was easier for him to live with himself.

One of his many fights with John turned violent. I was home alone with the two boys. I had to call the sheriff to stop them.

It was very frightening to see how violent Nick could be. The last fight he had with John, he beat him bloody. He was seventeen then and that was it. I could not handle his behavior anymore. I kicked him out. It was hard to do and painful for me. He lived with anyone who would take him in for a while. With him gone, the tension was gone also. Our family became what we call normal again.

Along with this strange behavior, I was just starting to see how sick his mind was. But it still did not really click. He would sneak girls into his room. We caught him about three times. As he got older, the girls remained young. The last one was twelve and Nick was seventeen. My husband kicked them out, but they were too drunk to go anywhere. They slept in my car. In the morning I had the girl come in and I called her mother.

Nick was fourteen when we began to have this trouble with him and these girls. So when school was out, I sent him to live with his dad in Rhode Island. John and I took him to the airport. When he left on the plane, I broke down and cried hard. John had to hold me. I almost collapsed. Nick thought he was only spending the summer with his dad, but I had arranged for him to stay and live there. I knew Nick was not coming home again.

I cried and cried. I knew I had betrayed Nick. He never would have gone if I told him the truth. I wondered how I could possibly save enough money to ever visit him or even go to his graduation. I need not have worried though. A friend of Nick's sent him enough money to catch the bus home. He lived with his friend for about a year before he returned home.

There are two other incidents that stick out in my mind that I would like to mention. Both of them happened when Nick was about seventeen. One evening, I came home from work late. I had worked nine or ten hours that day. When I came into my house, and I heard Nick screaming, "I want to die. Let me go! I want to die." He was down the hallway with John and John's best friend. Nick at that time was about 5'4" or maybe 5'5" and weighed 130 pounds. John and his friend were both over six feet tall and weighed about 180 pounds each. The both of them could not hold Nick down. None of them heard me come in. I went straight to my room and called the Sheriff. Nick got away from the boys, but the Sheriff found him on the highway and picked him up. They handcuffed him and took him to jail. A therapist from the mental health center evaluated him and sent him to the psychiatric ward at the hospital. He was kept overnight and released to me the next day. I did not talk to his doctor. I did not even see his doctor. He came home. That was that.

The other incident occurred one evening when Kristy and I were sitting on the couch watching TV. Nick came home. I said something like, "Nick, it's your turn for dishes." He just stared at us for the longest time, as though he hated us both. Then he went into his room and came out with his BB gun. He did not say a word. He just pointed it at us. He stared and stared at us. I remember thinking, "Thank God it's not a real gun. If it was, he would blow us away right now." All I felt was fear. I had never, never been afraid of my son. It was just a BB gun, but I felt real fear.

I began to think Nick must have a drug or alcohol problem. I began watching for signs of substance abuse. Was his problem serious, or would he straighten out in due time? No way did I have the money for inpatient treatment to save my son.

I went through drug and alcohol treatment with my brother and my youngest sister. It was pretty tough. I hoped I would not have to go through it with Nick. In all honesty, most of the time I did not see Nick's problem as something he or we could not control.

There was no way I could trust his real father to help me. At one point in time when I was very dumb and vulnerable, he sent me a Blue Shield card to pay all three kids' medical expenses, which would have been a big help. I used the card and not once was one bill paid. He got the checks in his name, cashed them, and kept the money. The kids had been in the hospital on several occasions. I owed thousands and thousands of dollars. It took a long time for me to get them paid off, but I did.

Nick also vomited when he was young. It started when he was in the third grade and continued until he was fifteen. His vomiting occurred about twice a year, usually in November or December and again around June.

Every time Nick vomited, he would vomit until his stomach and nose bled. He would then require hospitalization. He would be fed intravenously for a few days and the bleeding would stop. Once he had to have his nose packed also. Nick's doctor was in his seventies. He always said Nick had a virus. Now I am not so sure!!

Nick was still in his senior year when he went to court on the statutory rape charge. He went alone except for a person he had just met who befriended him.

Where is Nick today? On the very day Nick was to become a Marine, Nick was sentenced to 25 years in prison, with five suspended. Nick was alone that day and many days to come.

When I heard Nick's sentence, I fell apart completely. I screamed. I cried. I fell to the floor. I could not even stand up. I had thought the worst Nick would get was a couple of years at Pine Hills School for Boys. But Nick got prison. Prison. This could not be true.

The first time I saw Nick after he was sentenced, he was in the county jail. The pain a mother feels when she sees her son behind bars is indescribable.

What are we as a society doing to our children when we put eighteen-year-old children, babies, behind bars with hardened criminals? What are we doing?

My son has been there over a year, and he is no longer an eighteen-year-old boy. He has already seen too much for his young life.

Dear God—have mercy on our children.

✳ ✳ ✳

What finally triggered Kristy to reveal her story? Nick did. He was in his last year of school but he could not graduate with his class. He was just ten credits short, but he was eighteen years old. So he joined the Marines. He could still get his diploma. He gave me his Marine Corps certificate, and I kept it for him. I was so happy and proud of my son. He was going to make something of his life. I was on cloud nine. His success was all I ever talked about.

Kristy was feeling guilty, isolated, hurt, hopeless and suicidal. She told because she couldn't stand the unrealistic view I had of Nick. She desperately needed my support to deal with all of her pain.

Epilogue

How is Kristy now? Kristy is going to high school full time. She likes school and is getting good grades. It has been one year since she has been in the hospital. Things at home seem to be going well. Not perfect, but good. Kristy and her stepfather seem to have worked out a relationship of their own.

Kristy started vomiting two years ago. At that time, she weighed 130 pounds. Today Kristy weighs 100 pounds. She was going to the doctor every month to have her weight checked because her doctor wanted to watch for any problems with bulimia or anorexia. That was another scary thought for me to deal with. I was afraid that she may not stop losing weight. I often felt that Kristy thought that the more weight she lost, the better person she was becoming. Also, she is no longer the fat moose or fat cow that her brother used to call her. She has stopped losing weight and does not have an eating disorder.

Kristy has even worked out a relationship with Nick. She has talked to him on the phone without getting ill. Just a few months ago, she had her first visit with him in person with her therapist, Sandi. Kristy told him what kind of hell he put her through. She believed he was sorry for what he had done. She was then able to go on with her life. She has graduated from therapy now and is doing very well.

At the time of the disclosure, Kristy had just started going out with a new boyfriend. His name is Mike. Mike and Kristy are still going out. He has been very supportive throughout this ordeal with Kristy. He has helped her with a lot of the pain. I think it was helpful for her to have him care so much for her because at last she has someone who loves her for herself. Mike is seventeen and Kristy is sixteen. A lot of people think they are too young to be so serious. Who can say how old sixteen is after her years of abuse? She is advanced sexually, mentally, and physically. I will not judge her. I will trust that she knows what her feelings are. She alone knows what is inside of her.

Things have not worked out well between Kristy and her real father. He made a trip here with his mother this summer. Out of the two weeks he spent here, he only saw Kristy once. He took her out to dinner. He was to return the next day to spend more time with her, but that was the last time she saw him. After he returned home, he called her and tried to make her explain her ordeal to him in detail. That hurt her very much. She has not spoken to him since. Although it is painful, she is dealing well with it.

Kristy has had one crazy life put in front of her. How she has remained so sane and mature, I do not know. I pray I have had at least some positive influence on her life.

My poor baby. Kristy, I still love you and I always will. I know what he did to you, my baby. I know. I understand that you want me to know every horrible thing that he did to you. Well, my baby, I am sure that I have figured that out. So I will put it in black and white just for you. I love you, baby.

I am aware of the fact that when you were younger that your brother Nick bribed you with candy or cake or whatever it was. It does not matter. I still love you and I always will.

Kristy, I am ready to accept you as you are. You are still the you that I have always loved anyway.

Come Out of the Box

September of 1985. I moved to Seattle to attend college. I had become separated from my common law husband in July of 1984. My children had always exhibited sexual behavior, but after moving to Seattle it became more pronounced. While in college, I had been required to take a parenting class to enroll my youngest in the day care center at the college. The teachers were so good at teaching me how to handle other behaviors that I decided to ask for their help on the sexual behavior.

When I asked the social worker what to do, she took me into her office and closed the door. She proceeded to ask me questions for a half an hour about different things in the past. At the end of the half an hour, she told me that she thought my children had been sexually abused, and wanted me to think about who could have done this to them. In the meantime, she was going to make an appointment for me to talk to a counselor at the college.

It was like being knocked in the head, moving in mud up to my knees. I felt like my body went on automatic pilot and stayed there for several years. My ability to stuff my feelings is so good that I shut them all off and went through the motions, trying to keep my life and my family together. But the pain was so intense, and my loneliness and isolation so complete that I needed to get some of my feelings out. I kept a journal through most of the tough times just to vent some of my feelings.

❋ ❋ ❋

December 3, 1985. I met with a counselor named Marva at the college. She sounded very unconcerned, and referred me to a counselor at a women's center.

December 5, 1985—Met with Terri at the women's center. She was to become my counselor though I only saw her a couple of times. I talked to her for an hour and a half. She told me there was a 90 percent probability that my kids had been sexually abused. We talked about Jim, my ex. It was required by law that my children be evaluated by Child Protective Services to report the sexual abuse, but I decided to wait until after Christmas break to have the evaluation.

49

December 17, 1985—My kids were really getting out of control, tickling each other's vaginas fully clothed in front of people, once even in a grocery store. They were age four and six at this time, both girls. My youngest masturbated a lot.

I made an appointment with a psychologist in my home town for advice. He told me to remove her hand when she was masturbating, cuddle her, and stroke her arms and head. The masturbation was a type of self-stroking and I needed to give her a different kind. When there was sex play between my two kids, I needed to stop any behavior that leads up to it. They had kind of an almost maniacal laugh when they were being sexual. I learned to recognize that laugh. He also asked me if I'd cried yet or had trouble sleeping. I said no to both.

✳ ✳ ✳

Symptoms—my oldest: Tickles youngest's genitals while wrestling. Aggressive wrestling with my brother and Jim. Easily frustrated and crying. Told me she was afraid of being alone because she's afraid a monster would come in and take her away. Monster used to have a beard but doesn't anymore (after Jim shaved). I caught her trying to put phallic-shaped toy into my youngest's vagina when they were ages four and two while in the bathtub so I quit bathing them together after that. She had a vaginal irritation and rash for approximately one year, age two and a half to four. Jim moved in with us when she was two. She wet her pants to age seven.

Symptoms—my youngest: Sat on my hand. Masturbation on people's knees or furniture; voyeurism (I caught her peeking under dressing room door in clothing store watching total stranger get dressed, age four); exhibitionism; vaginal irritation and rash; came to me with vaginal smell on her finger and said, "Here, Mommy, smell this." Terrified of having her head laid back in the bathtub always.

✳ ✳ ✳

January 16, 1986. My oldest told me she was afraid of being alone because she was afraid of monster coming in and hurting her. She said he would hurt her and she would tell him to stop but he wouldn't. Her monster also used to have long hair and a beard but doesn't anymore. Her monster would sometimes hide in the bathtub, and she would go sit on him. She told me her monster wasn't here anymore. I asked if he was in Chicago and got no answer. Jim was living in Chicago at the time. Then I asked if her monster was Jim. She said her monster was her biological father, Fred. My youngest said her monster was herself.

I asked them later if the monster had told them I wouldn't like them anymore if they told me. They said yes. I told them I would always love them. If a monster hurt them, I would be mad at the monster, not them. They seemed surprised. My oldest keeps trying to change the subject.

I started thinking back through the last seven years of my life. My oldest was born in 1979. I had been living with her father for a year when I got pregnant. His alcoholism and mine, plus having a baby, put too much of a strain on our relationship. We split up when my oldest was five months old. I was very much in love with him. I felt like it had been my last chance at love, and that I had really screwed it up.

I met Jim in April 1980. My oldest was 14 months old when I met Jim. He moved in September 1, 1980. I had decided it was more important to live with someone who loved me than if I loved him. He quit his job September 15, 1980. I got pregnant October 1, 1980 when my oldest was one and a half. I had an IUD during my pregnancy. It was a very difficult, unplanned pregnancy. March 1981, Jim went back to work. My youngest was born June 20, 1981. My oldest's rash and wetting pants started. I had four jobs in six months. Jim quit his job and took another one. Jim got laid off June 1982 and started his own business. I started my own business. I took over all of the family, household, and financial responsibilities. I am eight years older than he. I was 27 and he 19 when we met.

We started having trouble getting along in October. He spent almost all of his time in the motorcycle shop. I became very depressed. We both did drugs and alcohol almost daily. He drank daily for the four years we were together with the exception of one six-week stretch.

December 1982—We took psilocybin, pot and booze to excess one night. When we got home, he wanted to sodomize me. When I told him no, he said he was going to do it anyways because I was too screwed up to stop him. He was too drunk to do it. I never trusted him after that. I avoided sex with him, or just "checked out" and shut my mind off. He became very jealous and possessive. From time to time after that, he would get very demanding for sex. Although he was never physically violent, he would bully me into it.

I always felt as though he was trying to move in with me from the time we met. He became very dependent on me for everything. The burden became really intolerable to me. I would try to break up with him but usually felt too sorry for him to do it because he was incapable of taking care of himself. I think he manipulated me more than I was aware of, into giving him money, letting him charge things or letting him stay. I tried very hard to stick it out, but he told me I wasn't trying hard enough. I started to catch him lying to me. He was so good at it, it took me a long time to catch on.

He was always very gentle, loving and playful with the kids. Although I saw the signs of sexual abuse, it never once occurred to me that it could be him doing it. Yet he was always horny and I could never give him enough sex. He couldn't control himself either. I changed my behavior so as not to arouse him because of his lack of control. It really scared me. He also disliked taking baths and brushing his teeth. He resented it when I asked him to.

I needed to get time away from him because he was so dependent and we were both working at home. I felt it was his responsibility to babysit for me. I now regret that. Whenever I went out with my friends, he was always waiting up for me. At the time I thought he was being possessive and checking up on me, but now I wonder if he wasn't molesting the kids and had to stop when I came home. I can remember one time clearly when I came home and got a creepy feeling, nothing specific, just gave me the creeps. Yet I ignored that feeling.

He came home one night at 3:30 in the morning extremely drunk. I had to get up at 5:00 to work. He wanted sex and he wouldn't let me sleep, and he wouldn't let me sleep, and he wouldn't let me sleep, and finally I told him to get it over with. I laid there and cried through the whole act. He either didn't notice or didn't care. I felt raped. I wasn't forced, but I still felt raped. I jumped out of bed when he was through. I told him it was over, I wanted him out of my house, and he was not going to talk me out of it this time.

He came and went for a couple of weeks, only to change clothes or take a shower, just to see if I'd change my mind, I think. I still went to bed with him once in a while. Being a good co-dependent, I couldn't stand to hurt him, but I didn't want to live with him either. I made it as easy on him as I could, still feeding him occasionally, sleeping with him occasionally, letting him see and babysit the kids, letting him wash his clothes there.

One night he came over after a two-week cocaine binge. I had the feeling if I didn't go to bed with him he would become violent. He was very agitated and demanding. I slept with him that night on the condition that he take a shower and brush his teeth. I never slept with him again.

He lived in his motorcycle shop for a year and a half in the rain and snow with no heat and no roof. He mooched off his friends, sold drugs, occasionally fixed a motorcycle, and eventually ended up living with a motorcycle gang in exchange for fixing their motorcycles. He ended up $50,000 in debt to the banks, well in excess of that amount in debt for drug deals. I think he eventually left town because of the number of people that were out to get him. He moved to Chicago to live with his biological parents. He's adopted. They paid for the plane ticket.

I used to get so angry and frustrated with him that I would hit him. I find that hard to believe now, but I did. He liked it. He'd smile when I slugged him. The worse I treated him, the more he seemed to love me.

After thinking back on all this, it seemed only logical to me that it had been he who molested my children.

January 8, 1986. Met with the social worker at Child Protective Services for the magical interview that was supposed to answer all my questions and tell me where to go with my problem. She interviewed both kids, found absolutely no evidence of abuse, and refused to see us anymore.

I called her a week later with my youngest's monster story. She referred me to a therapist at a children's services center, a counseling center specializing in children under the age of five. I felt more lost and hopeless than ever.

January 16, 1986. I met with Linda at the children's service center. I told her all my stories and she said she was alarmed. At least she took me seriously. It will cost me $20 an hour but at least I can get some help. They only see children five and under, but she agreed to see my oldest, too. We decided to work with the youngest first since she was more open and talkative.

I also found out I can't get financial help with this until one of them discloses who molested them. I'm going to college full-time with two kids and working 30 hours a week. Now I have to deal with this and nobody's going to help me pay for it.

January 20, 1986. My second counseling session with Linda. She said my youngest's play is very sexual with the dolls and she seemed to regress to baby behavior, which was unusual. My youngest masturbated a little on the dollhouse during the session. She told Linda that she had a ghost once that wanted her to be his wife but she wouldn't. She also simulated intercourse with the dolls.

January 24, 1986. I had nightmares about him molesting another woman's child so I told his biological parents. It was really hard. I hate having to explain to someone why I think he molested my kids, the details are so horrible. I wish I had proof.

I feel really confused. Sometimes I'm sure he did it. Other times, I can't believe he did it. I don't want to falsely accuse him, but I can't think of anybody else, and I don't want it to happen to anybody else.

Terri, my counselor, told me I may never know for sure. Some women have gone forty years without ever telling a soul. I tend to block everything out and pretend nothing has happened to my children. It's so painful to picture it that I stuff the feeling back and go on in numbness.

January 27, 1986. My third session with Linda. She said she is positive my youngest has been sexually abused. She told Linda a story about a man who tried to stab a little girl with a knife. Then the mom came home from the store and they got a divorce.

One day after we split up, Jim came to visit and brought a switchblade over. He wanted my oldest to push the button. I got very upset and made him put it away immediately, and wouldn't let my little girl push the button. At the time, I was more worried about her stabbing herself with it accidentally. Linda said it may have been a threat to keep the girls quiet.

Linda asked my youngest who this man was. She said, "I don't know. I wasn't there."

Linda also said today my youngest undressed the dolls, and one was a man and the other was a little girl. They were naked, and wrapped their arms around each other, and she said that they "splatted" on each other.

Linda said my oldest seemed much too mature and responsible for her age, contrasted with the fact that she still wets her pants. It's a cry for help.

She also said a lot of my youngest's play involves hot tubs, and that she's very stimulated by them. Is she masturbating there, too?

I can only guess what these stories mean. I am getting more and more upset and horrified all the time.

Jim called last night. I didn't talk to him very long. I told him I was having financial problems, so he said maybe he'd start sending me $20 a month. Big deal. He talked to the kids, too. I didn't say a word to him about anything. I don't know why.

January 28, 1986. Jim called again last night. A friend of his died over the weekend, overdosed on either alcohol or drugs or both. He was 34 years old. We talked awhile longer about him sending me money. He told me to keep reminding him or bugging him.

It's really hard for me to believe that we were so close, that he could do these terrible things, and that I never knew. He wrote the kids a letter, and at the end he said, "Be good or I'll beat you up." Is he really threatening them? Was the knife a threat and I didn't see it? I didn't read that part to them, but I'm going to give the letter to Linda the next Monday. I live for the therapy sessions, and I dread them at the same time.

I'm going into a no-money situation now. I may have to get a job and quit school or cut back.

I can't believe my oldest couldn't tell me about this. It hurts so badly that she couldn't tell me, but I also know that when it all started she couldn't talk. My youngest probably learned it from birth. I look at them now and it all makes sense. How could I be so close to such a monster? That marriage bond always gave him control over me.

February 3, session with Linda. I showed her the threat at the end of Jim's letter. She also thought the line about him getting up early every morning all by himself was a significant sign of his dependency. I also told her about his five little tickle fingers game that he used to play with the kids. He'd grab them by the collar, shake his fist in their face, and say, "You know what this is?," real mad like, and then "Five little tickle fingers," and tickle them. He also used to call himself a tickle monster.

My youngest told the counselor a story about her being the mom. She had two daughters who were playing with each other's privates all of the time and driving her crazy. She told Linda she had to lay on her daughters to protect them. Linda asked, "From who?" and she said, "Their dad." Linda asked her if she and her dad had any secrets from Mom. She said yes, but the only secret she'd tell about was my oldest's birthday present.

She may also ask me to get a physical exam for the kids in the near future to see if there was any physical damage done to them.

I've often read that offenders were sexually abused themselves. I can't believe Jim's folks are capable. But then I think about a friend of Jim's named Frank. It's always seemed strange that a man of his age, forty, would hang out with young teenage boys. Jim was twelve when he started hanging out with Frank when Frank was 35. I never did like the guy. He took advantage of Jim a lot, hiring him to work and never paying him, borrowing tools and keeping them. I remember a twelve-year-old boy hung himself in Frank's back yard a couple of years ago. Jim learned to drink with Frank, used to steal for him, and even went out one night with Frank to kill somebody. They didn't do it, though.

February 4, 1986. I had a very vivid dream about confronting Jim last night, mostly him laughing and thinking the kids' behavior was cute. It was a family picnic. Everybody was listening and he tried to act like nothing was going on. I was also beating him with a stick. Sometimes no words would come out, but I was really angry. So I asked him to at least tell me what he did to them. He said he was just really hurt and upset, and so he told the kids that if they wanted to make him feel better. . . And then I woke up.

The insomnia is really bad now. Between my nightmares and the kids', I hardly ever get a whole night's sleep. I work until I'm ready to drop and then smoke dope but it doesn't help.

February 11, 1986. Today was my oldest's first real session. She drew pictures and told stories about them. There is a difference between her monster and her ghost. The ghost is the one who comes in in the middle of the night. There was a picture where the girl's brother watched through the door. The ghost brought his buddy with him sometimes. That really scares me. She told Linda that her monster and my youngest's were different. That's something I have to think about. She said the ghost had a crystal ball. He could see and hear everything she said. If she told, he'd send his troopers to get her and take her to the place where he hides. My daughter thinks he's magic and that's why she's so terrified. Linda told me she'd never seen such a high level of fear in a child. It made her really angry.

When Jim and I were fighting after we split up, he told me that he had ways of always knowing where I was, what I was doing, and who I was with. He said if I had another man, he'd leave him in a pool of blood on the porch. It sounds like the same story.

I told my oldest yesterday that I knew this had happened, that I still loved her, that I wasn't going to leave her, that I wasn't going to leave her alone with the monster ever again, and that I knew she might not want to tell me but she could tell Linda. Maybe that's why she was so open today.

Linda said my daughter may have a bad week. I sure hope not. She's a holy terror to be around for a couple of days after the counseling sessions.

March 6, 1986. Meeting with Linda yesterday. My oldest said the crystal ball is electric. My youngest said Mommy touched her privates with garbage. Linda said she doesn't believe that I molested them. Thank you. My oldest is terrified to have a session with my youngest.

My oldest had a bad dream last night. She usually has nightmares the night after a counseling session. She was riding a horse. A man with a knife tried to stab her. The knife was small but very sharp. I asked her if it was the kind that you pushed a button and the blade came out, and she said yes. She said, "That's why you made Jim put his away, because it was so dangerous. But now he sold it."

March 9, 1986. I went to a meeting with a friend to a group called Adult Children of Alcoholics. That was like they'd been following me around all my life when they described the characteristics. Mostly that I don't express my emotions, I'm a people pleaser, reactor rather than actor. I am a perfectionist and a workaholic. I'm terrified of abandonment in a relationship but I seek out men who will abandon me. I've had relationships with thirteen different alcoholics in the last ten years based on sex, drugs and alcohol. I think I'll go to ACOA for a while and see if I can learn anything.

A lot of my kids' behaviors may be a reaction to having two alcoholic parents. I am alcoholic and drug addicted also.

New rules: No more secrets.

I came in the living room the other day and caught my oldest with her hands in my youngest's crotch swinging her around. My oldest panicked and ran out the door saying she had to go practice her racing. When I went outside, she was flat against the house on the porch just terrified. I tried to calm her down. I got her back in the house to play a card game, but didn't directly talk to her about it. Why do I have such a hard time directly talking about things?

I went through a period where I was real angry with my oldest for what she did to my youngest. I just couldn't stand to be around her and was real short-tempered with her. My counselor told me that I didn't need the extra guilt of feeling angry at her. She suggested spending time alone with her to get past it. It's so hard to get alone time with either one of my kids when I'm a single parent.

I decided I was transferring my anger at Jim to my oldest. I imagined wrapping my anger up in a box with wrapping paper and a bow and giving it back to him, and that seemed to help.

March 18, 1986. Happy St. Patrick's Day. I didn't go out. I started going to ACOA, and seem to have lost my zest for alcohol. It does make me crazy. I'm feeling less need to be perfect.

I went in for some counseling yesterday with Terri. It really did me good. There are an awful lot of things I never talk about. I need help dealing with the alcoholic influence and the sexual abuse.

I was worried about my inability to confront Jim. Terri told me when I really believe he did it, I would have no problem. I guess I am still denying it.

It's also spring break. I really need a rest.

May 26, 1986. It's been a long time since I've written. About two and a half months ago, I confronted Jim, his Mom and his aunt. It was very painful just having to repeat the details to people. I talked to Jim for an hour and a half on the phone. Basically what he said was "I didn't do it. Whoever did it is still out there and he might do it again. You'd better be careful." I told him everything I knew. He can't think of anybody else who could have done this. He said he told his Mom he was behind me all the way because I thought I was doing the right thing. I think he's a pathological liar and alcoholic sex deviant who raped both my babies for three to five years, and deserves to die a very slow and painful death. (Boy it felt good to write that.) Yet it took every ounce of willpower I had not to apologize to him when we were talking on the phone. I'm proud of myself for not apologizing.

I really doubt he's going to do any time for this. I'd like him to at least be arrested. I think he should have "sex offender" tattooed on his forehead in red so the innocent can see him coming.

I consider the possibility of his friend Frank being involved with molesting my kids and I'm really terrified. He's the kind of guy that might try and kill my kids for talking. I really believe he's that kind of person. We've been in therapy for six months now and no disclosure yet. It's really discouraging.

June 4, 1986. We haven't had an appointment for therapy for two weeks now and I don't know why. It really bothers me.

My oldest told me that nobody likes her at school or will play with her. She likes to be in a corner alone and talk to the wall and the wall talks back to her. That really scares me, too.

Our neighbor was shooting his gun off the other day. My oldest wet her pants. She told me it scared her and she wet her pants when he shot the gun. My youngest was real upset all that evening, she was laying under the table during dinner crying and yelling, "I want Jim to sit next to you." It seemed real odd.

I did take the kids to a free clinic downtown to get a physical examination to see if there was any physical damage done because of the abuse. I blindly trusted that any doctor anywhere would have some tact and gentleness, and that was a big mistake. He interrogated them and actually did an internal examination. He totally scared the hell out of both of them. I'm really sorry I did that. He found no physical evidence, by the way.

July 28, 1986. Time and therapy drag on. It's coming close to the time when I will graduate from college. I've started packing and moving. I decided to end the therapy. I'm going to miss our counselor a lot.

I've still been going to ACOA. My mother was hospitalized while we were home on vacation and went into DT's, admitted she's an alcoholic and is getting treatment. ACOA really helped me to deal with it all. My awareness has started to open up a lot of the secrets as far as the kids go. I started going to Al-Anon group because they had an Al-Atot group next door. They're AA family groups for families of alcoholics. It's real good for me to look at my past relationships with alcoholics even though I'm not in a relationship now. I'm alcoholic, child of an alcoholic, co-dependent, drug addicted and probably sex addicted. The only thing I've never been addicted to is cigarettes and heroin, probably because I knew I'd get hooked.

The kids had one really loud session last week, screaming "No, no, Daddy," and such, but Linda said they asked her not to tell me so we'd talk about it the next time. I asked my youngest what they'd talked about. She said it was the night Jim and I broke up. He'd made my youngest go to bed and my oldest stay up. She said the sound kept her awake. Then she said she didn't hear anything because she was asleep. I thought hooray, they're finally going to start talking about it. When I talked to Linda, she said they hadn't told her that story at all. They were just playing bar. So she's going to interview my oldest again this week and see what comes out. Otherwise she's just going to wind it down and set a definite date to end seeing my girls for when we move back to my home town.

My kids told Linda that one of my brother's friends had touched their privates inside their clothes. She was ready to call the cops on him immediately until I explained that they had only met him once for ten minutes, and that my brother and I were both there at the time. Why did they tell her that?

September 8, 1986. Linda got my youngest to talk about the incident again. She asked her if she'd heard my oldest crying, and she said no, laughing. But of course she was asleep and didn't hear anything. Then she said, "But Jim doesn't do that to her anymore." She wouldn't say what he didn't do anymore. I wonder if he mostly molested my oldest and my youngest watched?

Anyway, Linda has set a date for the therapy to end. We have two more sessions and that's it. I had planned on being done with school by now but I'm not, so we'll have to stay here but can't continue the therapy because Linda has been working with the children on saying good-bye and feels it's important that the therapy end as had been planned. I'm angry about that but it is my fault. They are just beginning to talk, and we have to quit.

Plus my mother died today. My father has decided to cremate her without a funeral, so we won't be going back. He seems to think he can handle everything okay. It feels so strange, one day she's here and the next she's not. I never got to say good-by.

My brother went home to be with my father, and I guess the two of them took my mother's ashes out to the graveyard in a cardboard box, and buried her in the family plot, just the two of them. It seems so cold. She deserves better than that.

September 29, 1986. I called Support Enforcement today. I've been trying to garnish Jim's pay checks for child support because I need the money desperately. Anyways, they told me he denies being my youngest's father. The paternity affidavit that I have signed and notarized is no good because he says he signed it under duress. So I have the choice of paying $300 for the blood tests and having the hearing now, or waiting until January and Illinois will pay for it. If he's found to be her father, they'll order him to pay me back the $300. I think my chances are nil of getting money from him so I'm not going to pay the $300 for the blood tests. I think I'd rather he weren't her father legally than have the child support. It's really going to hurt her if she finds out.

I told him he couldn't talk to the kids until he got a sex offender evaluation. He said he would, but he never has as far as I know. Linda told me that if she knew for sure that Jim did molest the kids that she wouldn't allow phone contact at all.

December 19, 1986. Jingle bells. I'm almost done with college. I've been working here for a firm part-time while I finish, and gaining some work experience. It's nice to have some money coming in.

Jimmy is at it again. He quit his job, moved to Tennessee with a friend, and didn't even say good-by to his mother. He was adopted and his birth mother found him when he turned 21. So after all those years of not having him, to having contact with him, to having him come to live with her, and then to leave like that must really hurt. Odd that he left about a month before the state would pay for the blood test. His birth family in Chicago won't speak to me or answer my letters anymore. They must have decided that it would be less painful to just end all contact with us and Jim. That seems really cold, too. I miss them. It's hard for my youngest to understand that she can't talk to her grandparents, aunts and uncles in Chicago anymore.

We're not going to therapy now.

✳ ✳ ✳

January 1, 1987. Happy New Year. Boy the last year was really rough.

My youngest had a bad dream last night. She said a drunk man was pinching her arm and hurting her with a skinny finger which she said was the middle finger. She was changing her clothes and forgot to go in the bathroom and he grabbed her. She said the man looked like Jim's brother-in-law without the mustache. He looks an awful lot like Jim. We hadn't even met his brother-in-law until a month or so ago.

Jim by the way is still in Memphis, unemployed and living with his friend, his friend's wife, and their two kids. Protect them, Lord.

We had an absolutely rotten Christmas. It was the first Christmas without my mother, and we were staying with my father. My father was in a bad mood, criticizing and yelling at us constantly. He's always been alcoholic and verbally abusive, and paranoid. I finally told him I didn't want to stay if he was going to keep yelling at me, and he told me he thought I should leave. It's the first time in my life I've ever told him I don't like being yelled at. When I found myself crying in the bathroom and my oldest crying in the back bedroom because of his behavior, I decided I don't have to take it anymore. So we came back to Seattle a week early. The peace and quiet was really nice.

Somebody suggested that I apply to Social Security Disability for financial help with the counseling bills. I'm going to start the paperwork for that soon. I have to sell just about everything I own in order to be financially eligible. Then we have to go for some psychiatric evaluations.

We're still not in therapy.

February 7, 1987. I finally graduated from college. I got the job I wanted in my home town and am moving back.

We went for the psychiatric evaluations to apply for SSI. The first one was for my oldest with a counselor SSI picked out of the phone book. He listened to my story and told me the only thing I needed to do was find a nice man and get married. Thank you very much for solving all my problems. He retired without writing a report, so we ended up being evaluated again. This time the same guy evaluated both of my kids. He was much nicer. He told me that he thought they would be okay until they got into puberty, and then we might need some more counseling, but they weren't emotionally disabled. It sounds nice, but I don't quite believe him. So after jumping through all those hoops to get SSI, I still don't get any financial help.

We're still not in therapy.

April 1987. We're back in the home town. Jim moved back right after we did. Jim's sister's husband babysat for us and left the kids alone with Jim for a while. My oldest didn't sleep a wink for three solid nights after that. So I put her on a waiting list with a mental health center. I don't know how long it will be.

I want to stay close to his family because I have no other support in this town, but I can't seem to avoid my kids seeing Jim when his family is taking care of them for me. I've talked to his sister but she doesn't believe me. She won't keep him from seeing them. There's no way I can bring myself to tell his adopted parents. They're so innocent and very religious. I hate to take his family away from my kids now because they're all we have in the way of family. They are my own family, too. They're good friends and I care a lot about them. But that means he still has contact with my kids.

September, 1987. We got a call from the mental health center to start my oldest with a counselor. Janet is a graduate student. Because of that, we don't have to pay for the counseling. This is the first time I've ever gotten any financial help with it, which is good because I'm still paying for the therapy in Seattle after a year.

She gets along real well with my daughter. I'm just going to put my oldest in counseling right now. I can't afford both, and I'm afraid she needs it more.

I tried to get medical insurance for my family and was turned down. The reasons given were that I am a former drug addict and because my daughter was receiving mental health counseling for sexual abuse. I feel like I'm being punished for my past and for telling the truth.

June, 1988. We've been in counseling nine months this time around. The kids still haven't told me who molested them, but my oldest has told me that she thinks Jim was the most likely person, and she wants to keep going to counseling to help her remember.

After we'd been had counseling for about eight months, my oldest and I had a long talk. I told her about how Jim had raped me and how he made me feel. She was really upset because nobody believed her that she hadn't been molested. So I told her all of the reasons that I thought she had.

That night she came into my room and told me that she had molested her sister. Apparently it was at my parents' house one night while I was out getting drunk and they were babysitting. My Mom was probably drunk and my dad passed out. My oldest said that she woke my youngest up and offered her a quarter to do it. My youngest said no. So she offered her fifty cents, and my youngest said okay. But she never paid her. My oldest mentioned something about the pencil-in-the nose trick, which is how she would wake my youngest up. She told me that she thought that's what you were supposed to do to babies.

Janet seemed to think my oldest is too young to be an offender, but she certainly doesn't care how my youngest feels about it. My youngest just covers her ears or hides when I try to talk to her about it. She's six now. The first thing she said was, "Then she owes me fifty cents." I told her that we don't sell our bodies, and she said okay.

This is the first thing concrete that has ever come out of the counseling. Janet's internship is up now, and we have to start with a new counselor in a couple of weeks.

I'm really angry about that even though I knew it would be that way from the beginning. How can we get anywhere if we have to keep changing counselors?

Janet did get me to start going to a support group for other women in my situation whose children have been molested, and many of them have been molested themselves. I'm learning that a lot of my behaviors are as if I was molested as a child, but I don't remember it. The group has been real good for me, as mother, daughter, woman.

In September of 1987, I started the AA program and began to deal with my alcohol and drug problems. I took the long way around to get to me, but I've been sober and straight for a long time. I'm still single. I don't know if I'll ever trust a man again. I don't think I ever trusted one before either. I see lots of progress for my family, learning how to be angry, how to make mistakes, and how not to keep secrets. We're all learning to have fun without going to bars. I hope that I found out and took action soon enough that my kids will have even half a chance at a normal life. Hopefully break the cycle of alcoholism that's been running in my family for so long. Alcohol didn't cause the abuse, but it certainly set it up and allowed it to happen.

Feelings are the hardest. I try not to stuff them but it's an automatic response and happens so fast that I'm not always aware of it. I avoid conflicts at any cost and that's not good for my relationships. Thirty-five years of feelings are beginning to come out now. When they do, it's like an explosion. I am self-destructive. I am working hard to treat myself the way I deserve to be treated and to insist on being treated that way by others.

I've had problems staying sober. I've been working on it for three years now, but I've been off drugs for a year and a half, and have not had one drink in six months now. That feels good. I'll never be cured, but I've made the decision not to drink. My life is sane most of the time now. When the insanity comes back, it doesn't last very long. I never want to go back to the cold, unfeeling stoned-all-the-time life I used to live, but the change is hard.

My kids are so much happier and easier to deal with it's incredible. They've told me they didn't know the secret touching was wrong, and they'll never do it again. My oldest wrote this poem:

> *Don't tell no one*
> *I have a secret*
> *Run away*
> *Escape from the monster*
> *Can tell no one*
> *Today I tell you*

My kids graduated from therapy after three and a half years. Now it's my turn, and I'm procrastinating but have finally begun. They can't change if I don't. Of course, I still don't have any proof that Jim molested my kids. The Legislature is working on a bill now that will change the statute of limitations so that if they do remember he can still be charged. I had to admit to myself that there was nothing I could do to punish him. I've left it in the hands of my Higher Power. It's been difficult to let go of that anger and it's far from being all gone.

I wish I could end this story, but it's a story that will have no end. At an ACOA conference, we were to ask our Spirit Guide for help with where we were stuck, and then to write down whatever came into our heads. I'll close with that letter and his answer.

✳ ✳ ✳

How can I grow more? I feel stuck and unable to feel pain, joy, sorrow. I'm a little girl with pigtails, shut up in a little white cardboard box, curled up safe and protected. If I and my feelings come out of the box, I can be hurt and frightened. If no one sees or knows how I feel, I am safe. The feelings are all bottled up tight with a cork and wax, and if I uncork them even a little, they'll explode, and then everyone will know my shame and grief. I need to feel a conscious contact with my Higher Power, that I can trust him to protect me and show me the way to go.

"Open the box. Uncork the bottle. Free the pigtails. Throw it all to the wind, and let the rain wash you clean. Then the Higher Power can reach through the garbage to hold and nurture you. Forgive yourself. Fear is the mind killer and paralyzes your emotions. Fear not, for I am with you."

Silence

Born of assault to the body, the mind, the emotional soul! Bred in fear, in guilt, in pain. Suffered alone.

Silence, choking me, imprisoning me. . . . I had found the strength to survive my own sexual abuse when I was a child and to go forward out of the pain. I fight now for the strength for a way to help my own child, a victim of the same crime. Yet—almost —I did not have the strength to shatter the silence by putting pen to my story. Not until I lay in my bed during the early morning hours, unable to sleep, did that Silence become synonymous with our offenders. Breaking it became symbolic in my mind of another path towards healing, towards positive change.

✳ ✳ ✳

The evening I discovered that my ten-year-old daughter had been sexually molested brought a name to the knot of fear and anxiety I had carried inside me for months. The truth of what my daughter had suffered ripped through me. For the last few months I had suspected something was wrong. It was just a gut feeling. There had been subtle changes in her behavior. She had begun having trouble at school with her work and with her friends. She seemed to distance herself from me, becoming moody and unpredictable at times. I had talked to her teacher. She had noticed a difference also.

That particular evening, my daughter, Lea, and I went for a walk in the neighborhood with the dog. In the course of our conversation, she gave me a "what if" situation about an older neighbor man. At that moment, I knew the rest of the story in my heart. She did not tell me anything had actually happened. I was faced with "What do I do?" There was never any question in my mind, then or later, about believing her. Nor was there any question as to why she didn't tell me. I knew all those answers from my own childhood abuse, answers like, "It was my fault. I did something wrong. I don't want to cause any trouble for Mommy. She won't love me if she knows. Something bad will happen—like he warned me," and on and on.

I did question in my own mind why I didn't recognize what was happening. It is a question that haunts every parent of a victim. It was the same one my mother asked herself when I finally told, many years later when I was an adult. I believed I would never let my children be hurt like I was. I could keep my Lea safe. My daughter asked me later if I felt guilty. I could not say yes to her, but inside my head, I was screaming "Yes!" I felt so responsible.

I am a single working parent. That year I made the decision that Lea would remain home alone after school, another latchkey kid. I did not allow her friends over when I wasn't home. With no siblings, she had only her dog to keep her company after school. We would talk to each other by phone each day after she arrived home. I was unhappy with the arrangement, and I attributed some of Lea's changes to this. The child support had long since stopped coming. There was no nearby relative I could turn to for assistance, and no other reasonable alternative in our neighborhood. Besides, I told myself, I was only twenty minutes away at my job. We lived in a "nice, clean, safe" neighborhood.

On the job, I was trying desperately to prove myself for promotions which in turn would make things better for us financially. I was trying to be a good mother and father to my daughter. There was seldom time left over for my own needs. I had no desire to find someone to remarry. I didn't want to bring home a stepfather for my Lea. One of my offenders had been a stepfather. I was not taking that chance with her. I was coping and doing the best I could to spread myself across my responsibilities.

Oh, God, why? Why this little girl who had brought so much into my life? We had adopted Lea when she was barely one. She had brought so much depth and width to our lives. She was such a beautiful, happy, loving child. When we brought her into our family, it was a promise for a good life. We were raising Lea to know that she was adopted. We shared as much of her past with her as we knew, trying to develop roots, continuity, and self-esteem within her.

As a small child, Lea had such a bubbly, happy laughter, one that was filled with the innocence, freedom, and trust of youth. After my divorce, the laughter came less often. The sadness in her eyes came more often. When our marriage broke up, like most children, she felt his leaving was her fault in some way. Maybe she had done something; maybe he no longer loved her; maybe she really didn't belong; maybe she wasn't really his. When he quit calling, writing, or even sending cards on birthdays; when he tried to totally drop out of her life; her self-doubts and the loss of her father's love were reaffirmed. My family is small. There was no male relative to pick up the role and fill the void in her life.

The pedophile who molested my daughter knew exactly how to select and groom his victims. Similar to his previous victims, my daughter came from a single parent family. The head of the household was a working mother. She had no siblings and no father figure in her life. She was trusting and open, and at that time a latchkey kid. Each pedophile may have a different pattern. This seemed to be his.

He was a married, church-going member of the community, retired, with time on his hands to befriend neighbors in need, and their children. He gave the appearance of a nice old man that one could trust. This was supported by the invitations from him and his wife to visit their home, have coffee with them, and ask a favor of them if one was ever needed. They had children and grandchildren of their own. They knew "raising a family isn't easy."

Parents try to teach their children to believe in themselves and in other people. While they must be cautious and be aware of what could happen, life is basically good, and so are the people in their lives. Then some bastard like this one comes along to disprove that. When Lea was small and we went camping, I could identify the dangerous animals for her and warn her. I had no way of identifying this one.

When faced with what had happened to Lea, I was filled with anger towards the offender, and overwhelmed with decisions and responsibilities. I felt the need to be calm and reassuring for my daughter's sake. I also felt the need to be outraged, vindictive, violent towards the animal who did this to her. I was faced with dealing with her pain, my family's pain, and the pain of what had happened to me so many years ago. Old wounds—new wounds—same crime. "When and where, if ever, does it end?," I asked myself.

That night after our walk, I hugged my daughter and told her I loved her. I wanted to take away her pain and knew I could not. When I went to bed, I could not sleep. By the next day, I had made the decision to call our local police. Fortunately, the department had a special task force for crimes involving child abuse. The detective who visited us that afternoon was a female specifically trained for this type of case. She took Lea into a bedroom where they talked for a couple of hours.

When they emerged from the room, I was not surprised to have the detective confirm my suspicions. She was kind, calm, and reassuring to my daughter. I was not prepared, however, for the question that she asked my daughter just before leaving that day. In closing her visit, she asked Lea if she felt safe staying there with me or if she feared I would get angry and hurt her because of what had happened. She assured Lea she could go with her to a safe place if she was afraid of me. At the time, I was hurt and furious. I stood there in disbelief, unprepared to hear this. The thought to harm my daughter, or the thought that she could be taken from my home had never occurred to me. Now I realize it was a question that needed to be asked for Lea's safety. Lea wanted to stay with me.

Faced with decisions, I elected to press charges. The offender was arrested and released on bail. He remained at his home, free to go about the neighborhood until trial—a period of almost a year. When I replay in my mind all that happened in those many months between filing charges and the trial, the trial itself, and Lea's pain, I still question whether my choice to press charges was right. I could have left the state (like his victims' parents before us). I could have blown him apart with a shotgun. I knew she felt her dad would shoot him had he been there. I believe what I did was right. However, the end did not seem to justify the pain and suffering that was Lea's throughout this legal process.

There were a number of assistant district attorneys in our district. I refused to have a male working on the case. We were assigned a female who had a long track record. She was known for her outstanding abilities in working on sexual assault cases. It looked hopeful. On our visits to the DA, my daughter met with her alone. It was easier for Lea to talk about what happened without me there. In my heart I knew why, but it hurt. I wanted to be near her. No videotapes were made of these sessions. Our state had recently passed legislation allowing tapes if the victim was eight or younger. By the time we were at this stage, my daughter was over that age limit.

Shortly into preparation of the case, we were assigned another DA, again female. Before reaching pretrial, a third female DA took over the case. Even though the state had enacted vertical prosecution in such cases (which assured the same lawyer will handle each case in its entirety), Lea had to retell her story and work with three different ones. Each one was lost to us through reassignment to other courts and other cases.

The DA's office and the detective on the police force worked together to bring the case to court. They were responsive and understanding to my questions and concerns. However, both of them assured Lea that once she testified and the trial was over, she could forget about all "this." It would be behind her. To propose that the abuse can be forgotten, put away, shut out, is untrue. It was an honest error on their part, an unknowing lie. The difficulty these comments caused in the counseling process and later in our own discussions is hard to describe for Lea even today. Victims must deal with the facts and the painful feelings surrounding the sexual abuse over and over again, in counseling, in healing, in surviving. Victims never forget. We can learn to survive, to stop being a victim, to be in control. Yet the pain, the memory, is always there. These hopefully become less intense, less disruptive as we move on in our lives.

During our investigation, we learned that the offender had been arrested on several other occasions but never brought to trial before. I asked myself if these parents had been wiser than I, if they had known what it would be like. Was I right?

I was to find that other neighbors knew this bastard was a child molester. Oh, God, if only someone had stepped forth to shatter the silence and tell me about him when we moved to that neighborhood. Or if only the law provided for a method of making pedophiles known to their community. I believe our children's right to protection overrides any right the offenders may have. When our case came to the courts, I wanted to sit in front of the offender's home, on the public sidewalk, with a sign stating the facts—that he was a child molester. I was told that should I do that, he could file civil charges against me. I was angry. I was driven with that anger, needing to do something! Yet I felt bound and gagged.

There was a Victim's Assistance Division in our state. However, I only found out about them after inquiring through the detective for resources and referrals to get counseling for Lea. This division seemed under-trained and overloaded, with ill-defined objectives. After many phone calls, complaints to supervisors, and letters to the DA, communication with the Victim's Assistance Office became somewhat easier.

During the trial, the courtroom was "open court." I had asked for a "closed court" and been denied. I have yet for anyone to explain to me the benefits provided by open court in the hearings involving child sexual abuse. Because I was a witness in the case, I could not be in the courtroom during the trial. I could not be there for my physical presence, at least, to provide support to Lea during her two days of testimony. Yet because of the defendant's legal rights, she had to sit facing him during her entire testimony. When I was finally called to testify, my daughter was sent from the courtroom to stand alone in the hall. She waited and suffered alone again. I could see her through the door window, my heart aching while I stared at her offender, giving my testimony. No one was there from the Victim's Assistance Office to sit with her. I had not brought a friend to help, out of respect for Lea's need to keep our friends from knowing about the sexual abuse.

The last day of trial, I came alone to the courtroom, to hear the summaries and await the court's decision. I sat across from the defendant's wife, who had testified to her husband's innocence. How warped was she, or how involved? Then I saw her husband. I struggled to calm the rage inside as I stared at the bastard. I had been writing comments or names I called this animal in my head, expressing the anger I could not scream out to the judge. A trial deals only with facts—right! How does one bring forth to the courtroom the "evidence" of the emotional and psychological pain and damage caused by sexual abuse of a child?

The court found the offender guilty on several felony counts. My daughter had held up well during the two grueling days of testimony. They believed her. They knew he was guilty! Yet the judge deferred sentencing until "the defendant can be psychologically evaluated by the State to determine if he is mentally and physically capable of surviving a prison term." My mind screamed, "Hell, Judge, he has been found mentally and physically capable of molesting my daughter!! Is that not enough?" Even though it could not be used against this bastard, the judge knew he had been arrested before for molesting children! What would it take to get this man removed from society? "What?" I silently screamed.

Upon completion of the incarceration for evaluation, the defendant was returned to court for sentencing. I went to observe even though it was not required. I needed to be there, to hear the results . . . the State found he was not a threat to society, and that physically, he might not endure a long prison sentence. Based on those findings, the judge sentenced him to one year imprisonment and several years probation. I sat there asking myself, "Does it make a difference that the judge is male, an older male?" The time actually served by this man was less than five months in a minimum security environment.

This animal committed sexual assault. He violated the body and the trust of a child. He robbed her of her childhood innocence, of her very belief in herself. He stole her trust and faith in me as her protector. No sentence or restitution can resolve, replace, or repair the damage caused a victim and the victim's family in this crime. It is one far worse than armed robbery, assault and battery, fraud, etc. It is a crime which in many instances robs a victim of many happy, healthy, productive years. One only has to read the statistics—or—be a victim to understand this. Yet our legal system continues to minimize the crime and discount the victims by handing down short, if any, prison sentences. This must change!

Even though I requested to know, we were not notified by the system when he was released to return to his home and to our neighborhood. I had been told by his probation officer that we had no legal right to be notified. The laws of protection apparently served the offender.

I wrote letters to the judge and to my state representatives. I contacted various organizations in an attempt to get this man removed from our neighborhood. I raged inside as I saw him walk freely up and down our streets. My God! How must Lea have felt? It was clear the court's decision regarding his short sentence reaffirmed to her that she was not valued. Being found guilty was not enough. The punishment did not fit the crime. In preparing for this trial, we—myself, the detective, the DA—had all encouraged Lea to testify so this person could be put away so other children would not have to go through what she did. The system made liars of us all. Yet, on more than one occasion, I was to hear, "At least he was convicted. He has suffered for what he did. Is that not enough?" Only those victims such as Lea and only families such as ours may really understand why that is not enough.

I had long before rearranged our home situation so that Lea was not home alone anymore. She was never allowed to play alone on our street anymore. There was still a knot of fear and anger as I watched this man upon his release from jail. He went about his life seemingly without fear, without an alteration to his activities. I knew my daughter felt the same fear, the same anger.

Finally, I made the decision to leave the area, to quit my job and to find a new place to begin again. It meant more losses for Lea. She left friends and familiar surroundings. She had to start in a new school. It meant more broken ties for her. Who would—who could she trust in the new neighborhood? Which neighbors? Which friends? It seemed we continued to be victims.

After filing charges, I sought counseling for Lea and for myself. We needed professional help to deal with all the issues, the feelings, and the long-term effects of sexual abuse. It had taken several tries before finding a counselor who I felt was the best to work with us, and who would wait for payment. At first, it had been difficult for me to confront these professionals who had multiple initials after their names and say to them, "I do not feel you are the right person to work with us," but I had to. Finding the right counselor is very important. Even then, it may not bring the results you expect or hope for. But I had to try.

The first time, we stayed in counseling for more than a year. The counselor gained little ground with Lea. My daughter still couldn't talk about her victimization or about her feelings, with the counselor nor with me. I worked with a separate counselor to try to understand how I could help my daughter through this time, to better understand her trauma, to resolve my own guilt, and to find the strength to move on and fight the battles.

Throughout this, I found myself dealing more and more with my own experiences as a victim and sorting through all the old stuff that suddenly didn't seem so old. Often the mountain seems insurmountable. The need to move on and to do something to survive is greater.

Finally the counselors suggested we take a break and let some time pass to see how things went with Lea and with me. It was important for the counseling to be a pleasant enough experience that if Lea later needed to return to counseling, she could draw from this experience and feel good about it.

For a while, things seemed to be going along okay. Lea made new friends in our new neighborhood. She was doing better in school. I wanted things to be better for her. I began to realize they were not. There were certain subjects we could not seem to discuss, certain words that were taboo—words and subjects that I knew must remind her of the abuse. Yet I needed to reach her. I knew our experiences of abuse had been different, but I hoped sharing my own experiences with her would help Lea avoid some of the problems I had suffered.

After Lea entered her teenage years, our relationship was nowhere near where I hoped it would be. Lea built the wall well. The wall was to shield her from hurt. The wall would keep anyone else from getting close enough to betray her trust, to cause her pain. She seemed so far away from me. No one, including me, had been there for her then. She needed no one now. I knew she felt that way.

During this time, Lea's dog, her childhood friend, became sick and was in a lot of pain. After taking the dog to our veterinarian and learning there was nothing that could be done for her, I had her put to sleep. This dog had been Lea's pal, her friend with whom she shared all her secret things she felt she could tell no one else. She had shared her pain suffered from the abuse with this friend. Shortly after she lost her dog, she blamed me. Later she blamed herself. It was not until much later, though, that Lea told me she felt it was her fault because the molester told her the dog would die if Lea told their secret. Just one more example of a control tool that pedophiles use.

As Lea began her high school years, the problems between us increased. Some seemed typical for the teenage years and some did not. It was difficult for me to sort through them and understand the difference. I was confused about how to parent. How much of this was related to the abuse? I felt the wall between us thickening, the distance increasing. Fear was once again grabbing at my guts.

Lea began skipping classes. Her grades dropped. She was changing friends. Her new ones were radically different. She began showing outright hostility and defiance towards me. Next came the running away. Our relationship was becoming a nightmare. Neither of us could seem to wake up. I was terrified of my daughter being on the streets. I found myself having to talk to police and having to admit I could not control my daughter in order for them to search for her. I needed answers and had none.

During this time, I tracked down my ex-husband. Lea knew I found him. She was repeatedly telling me she could not and would not live with me. After one of the runaway attempts, I finally offered for her to go and live with her father if he would agree. He was married and living over a thousand miles away. After all this time, it hurt to ask for his help. I did not want to do it. However, they agreed to give it a try. The "try" did not last long. In less than a month I got the call that Lea was coming back home. I felt that there was no room in his life for a troubled teenager. To me, it was simply another form of rejection, one that was to repeat itself whenever she reached out to him. What did she feel? How deep did it hurt? I do believe that as her father, he could have done so much to help her through the pain, through her healing process as a survivor. A healthy, loving father/daughter relationship can be replaced by no other. The absence of such a relationship is a painful void. I plead with every absentee father to think about this. I ask every father who is or has been an abuser to think about the relationship to which your child was entitled and of which you robbed them.

After Lea returned from her father's, the running away continued. I found myself again filing yet another police report. At times like these, I felt I must be doing everything wrong. I wept until there were no more tears. I felt so damned alone.

Finally, we returned to counseling. The counselors confirmed my belief that Lea's destructive behavior was directly related to the sexual abuse. Her hate and anger towards me was an expression of her pain. She was rejecting even herself. The anger and rage I had felt towards her offender was rekindled. I would awake in the night with an overpowering urge to go to his home and kill the bastard . . . slowly, in front of his wife! Yet I knew, as before, I had to see this through. I had to work it out and help Lea in whatever way I could, if she would let me.

This time in our life, in hers, is a story of its own—one that continues as Lea stands at the doorway of adulthood, about to pass through. She is becoming stronger as she works through her pain. Lea's road to survival will continue long past this current time. I know this inside for I have been there, traveling a similar road. As I watch my daughter struggle to break free of the crippling psychological scars of abuse, my mind's eye replays my own experiences and my own breaking free.

I have taught myself to be strong, to be independent, and to survive in spite of . . . because I knew I must. I wanted to survive. Yet no matter which outside self I let the world see, inside I have often felt I didn't measure up or didn't really belong. I haven't found my own place in the scheme of things. The sexual abuse I suffered as a child left feelings of being used, unworthy, alone, and invisibly separated from everyone else. In my relationships, I have unconsciously kept a bit of distance between myself and others. It's my own personal "wall" of protection. Many times I have felt there was unfinished business in my life, goals not achieved. Yet I have not reached out for my brass ring. Perhaps the ropes that bound me were the scars of abuse. There is so much pain and darkness before the light. It is the kind of pain I had prayed my own daughter would never have to suffer; the kind of pain my mother and I shared when I told her what had happened to me years later. Now I pray that my daughter's children will not have to suffer. I pray for an end to society's tolerance for the abuse of our children.

As I end my story, I would like to share something I apply to my personal life that I learned in the business world. Control is an important issue for a victim. It has been one for her and for me. So many times as an adult, I have felt I had absolutely no power to change the course of events. Realizing I cannot control the actions of others or the circumstances in which I find myself, I have learned that I can still exercise some influence in any situation by controlling the way I react! When I remember this, I do not feel as helpless. I am capable of determining my own reactions, deciding my own feelings, choosing my next step.

I can refuse to suffer in silence alone!

No Guarantees

I was wondering why Nolan wasn't home for lunch yet when the phone rang. I figured that was probably him to tell me why he was late or that he couldn't make it at all. He couldn't make it, all right; he was in jail. My world came crashing down around me.

A few days earlier, Nolan had told me that he had received a strange request from our ten-year-old son. Dan had asked him to please never wear that "towel" again. (It was a wrap-around that men wear when they step out of the shower.) He said that Penny, a seven-year-old neighbor girl, had told him that she couldn't come to our house anymore because every time Nolan wore that, she saw his "pee-pee." I was so angry and embarrassed when he told me this. How could he be so stupid? How could he care so little for his family as to risk putting us all through this embarrassment just for the sake of comfort? Why hadn't I been more adamant when I expressed my discomfort about him wearing that thing when there were other children in the house? How could I have been so weak? What if they blew this whole thing way out of proportion and Nolan ended up going to trial and maybe to prison?

When the phone call came, I knew that my worst fear had come true—Penny's parents had flipped out and blown this whole thing way out of proportion. What were we going to do now? Our lives could be ruined! No matter what the outcome, some people would always think that Nolan was a pervert. How could we ever face our neighbors again? What if Nolan ended up in prison for a crime he didn't commit?

I knew I didn't want to be alone with this. It was just too much to take. I called my friend, Diane, and was so very, very thankful when she answered the phone. After she arrived, I started a "seclusion" process that I know now was a healthy means of survival. I just didn't have the strength to explain this to the many people who might ask questions. I needed all my strength to just get myself and my son through this. I started cancelling appointments that I had that week. I closed all the drapes and Diane screened the phone calls. Within a few days, I also had the phone number changed.

That evening I went to the jail to see Nolan. It just so happened that it was a visiting day. I was allowed to speak to him for ten minutes through a window. My heart ached to think of what he was going through.

In the morning, I received a phone call from Penny's mom. She wanted to let me know how badly she felt for Dan, my son, and me. She also wanted to assure me that she knew I had nothing to do with it. I told her that I felt the whole thing had been blown out of proportion. I assured her that there was no malicious intent involved on Nolan's part.

Why would she be calling anyway? I figured that the real reason was just to ease her conscience.

Later that day, they set Nolan's bail. The judge asked me if I had any objections to him coming home. He kept saying the phrase, "because of the seriousness of the charges." I was so confused. What was he talking about? Then the next thing I knew, he was saying that when Nolan got out of jail, he was not to return to our neighborhood. He couldn't come home! This whole thing was becoming a bigger nightmare all the time.

When we left the judge's chambers, our lawyer asked me to come to his office. When I got there, he told me what the charges were. Then I asked him, "Can you please tell me what the charges are about?" He said, "I just told you." I said, "No. I mean why." So he handed me some papers to read. They were the report from the social worker, the description of the charges, etc. I remember thinking that I was glad there was a bathroom across the hall because I felt like I was going to get sick.

In the social worker's report, it described in detail how Nolan had molested the neighbor girl for the past six months. My common sense told me that a little girl could not make this stuff up. I suddenly realized why the judge had acted the way he had—these were the papers that he had read! Now the phone call from Penny's mom made sense, except for everything that I had said. Oh, I wanted to call her back, but the lawyer strongly advised no contact. I decided that I had better do what he advised.

The whole situation had changed. I now had to deal with the fact that there was a very real possibility that my husband was a child molester.

I believe now, looking back, I literally went into a state of shock. It was as though I was in a big bubble, and I could only focus on what was in that bubble. My friend, Diane, was in it with me, and everyone else was in the background. The lawyer was trying to give me some very simple instructions, but he finally gave up and gave them to my friend's husband to carry out. I simply could not stay attentive to him long enough to grasp what he was saying to me. He was not in the bubble.

I was able to discuss with Diane the "what if's." What if the charges were true? What if he went to prison? By the time Diane's husband returned from the errand, I could at least comprehend some of the details that I had to attend to next. However, I don't know what I would have done had I not had someone to escort me and do some thinking for me.

That was the worst day of my life. I was broken. I literally could not stand straight, and I could hardly talk. It just took too much effort. I cried almost constantly. I didn't know what to do. I even thought about suicide. When I got home that night, I knew I couldn't go on in my own strength. I cried out to God with all my heart to give me his strength.

When I woke up the next morning, I literally had a new strength. God had answered my prayer. I didn't feel the need to cry all the time, and I could talk freely now. I felt kicked, but I didn't feel defeated anymore.

I got Nolan out of jail that afternoon and took him to the motel where he could be staying for a while. Then I went to see the counselor that I had been seeing for the past eight months. This was the one appointment that I had not cancelled all week. I was surprised that she hadn't heard about Nolan being arrested, and when I told her about it, we both cried. Towards the end of the session, I was able to admit to her that I thought Nolan had done the things that he was accused of doing. I asked, "What do I do now?" She said I had to tell him. But she gave me hope. She told me that there were programs to help people like Nolan, and that the system would rather see him helped than put him in prison and throw away the key.

My biggest fear at that moment was that when I confronted Nolan, he would deny it. I figured I could handle anything except another lie.

When I confronted him, he admitted that he was guilty.

It's been over a year since I learned about Nolan's secret, and I've experienced a lot of pain, humiliation, and anger. But what I'd like to share now are what I feel are a couple of major victories I've had during this time.

When I was told that it wasn't smart or healthy to trust my husband anymore, I felt very confused. I always thought that trust was a very important factor in a good marriage. So I asked the Lord, "How can I stay in a marriage with a man I'm not supposed to trust anymore?" And just as clear as a bell He answered, "You can trust Me."

Oh, yes! If the Lord wanted me to stay in this relationship, then indeed I could trust Him. So that became a rule of thumb—I couldn't trust Nolan, but I could trust Jesus.

Another area that I just recently experienced victory in is one that again has to do with trusting the Lord with my future.

For many months I felt like running away. Just recently we moved from Montana to Oklahoma, and I was so thrilled. I finally got to run 2100 miles away from where the whole nightmare took place. Now I didn't have to wonder who knew about us, and I figured that now I would feel like I could settle down. I was wrong. As soon as we got to Oklahoma, I had an overwhelming desire to run back to Montana—to my folks—to people I could feel safe with.

I finally had to take time out, pray about this, and take a deep look inside to find out what was going on with me. Why did I keep wanting to run?

When the answer came, it was so very clear and simple. I was afraid of being hurt again. I was sure that if I committed one hundred percent to our relationship, everything would be jerked out from under me again. I just couldn't risk that.

But the freedom from this fear came when I realized that there is no guarantee of not being hurt in any relationship. We take risks in any relationship that we enter. This revelation put things in a whole different light for me! I'm now willing to work at my relationship with Nolan, and I even allow myself to be happy in it. I don't pretend that nothing has happened. I don't close my eyes to things around me. If I get a funny feeling that something isn't quite right, I don't tell myself, "Oh, don't be silly" anymore. I look into it. But I refuse to let fear of something happening again ruin my life. Fear is such a crippling emotion.

Looking back over the past fourteen months, I am reminded of the poem, "Footprints in the Sand."

> One night a man had a dream. He dreamed he was walking along the beach with the Lord. Across the sky flashed scenes from his life. For each scene, he noticed two sets of footprints in the sand; one belonged to him, and the other to the Lord.

> When the last scene of his life flashed before him, he looked back at the footprints in the sand. He noticed that many times along the path of his life, there was only one set of footprints. He also noticed that it happened at the very lowest and saddest times in his life.

> This really bothered him, and he questioned the Lord about it. "Lord, you said that once I decided to follow you, you'd walk with me all the way. But I have noticed that during the most troublesome times in my life, there is only one set of footprints. I don't understand why when I needed you most you would leave me."

> The Lord replied, "My precious, precious child. I love you and I would never leave you. During your times of trial and suffering, when you see only one set of footprints, it was then that I carried you."

How Did We Get Here?

In the courtroom just waiting. My husband is being tried for child molesting. The lawyers, my husband and the judge were talking back and forth. I begin to lose myself in thought. How did we get here? I start to recall it all.

The day after Thanksgiving, I had just walked in the house after work. He was real nervous and almost crying. "Hi," I said, noticing something wrong. "What is the matter?" I said over and over again. "I have to tell you something," is all he would say. I grabbed him, "Tell me what it is," I said. My mind was going in all directions at once. One of the kids was hurt bad? Something happened to my brothers or sister? Or someone died in the family? Almost shaking him, I said it again, "Tell me what it is, please." Looking at me and then at the floor, he said, "They called me to come down to the police station. I have been accused of child molesting." I stared at him. "What did you say?" I just knew I didn't hear him right. What was someone trying to do to him, to us, to my family? This just couldn't be. He started to tell me what the phone call was all about.

I was lost in a mass of confusion. None of this was making sense. I started crying. My insides were crying out all kinds of things. "How could you do this to a child? What is wrong with you? What made you want to molest a child anyway? What am I going to do? What about our children?" But I couldn't get anything to come out of my mouth.

The courtroom voices were penetrating my thoughts. "The court sentences you to a three-year deferred sentence to the mental health center," the judge was saying to my husband. I asked myself, "Just what does this mean?" From November to March seemed like a blur. We went to the mental health center. They were ready to help us, but I didn't know if I was ready. Going to the mental health center meant a lot of hard work, really looking at my feelings, being able to face facts about myself I didn't like, and also being able to accept some good things about myself.

Blame, guilt, shame, anger, frustration, being lost, were always someone else's words. Feelings, real true feelings, I would never allow myself to have. I am now trying to work on just accepting the fact that it is okay to feel, and then maybe to have someone to work out those feelings with.

I started to blame myself for everything that went wrong. Maybe if I could have seen that my husband was unhappy, I could have tried harder to make him happy. Over and over again I asked myself, "What could I have done differently? Was it something I was doing wrong in our sex life?" I tried real hard not to argue with him. I don't like arguing. Could that be the problem? When I discovered I wasn't to blame, I found more feelings to deal with.

As I started to deal with my anger about what my husband had done, I discovered a lot of feelings that I had locked up about my childhood.

I try to remember the happy times of my childhood. It seems like there were a lot of them when the memories first start off, but you see, my parents drank a lot. I remember a lot of fighting. It was screaming and calling names, sometimes hitting. I remember hiding my head under the pillow and talking to myself so I couldn't hear them. Because my parents were at the bar a lot, I had to watch my younger brothers and sister. This all started on a steady basis after the night I asked my parents several times if they would take us home from the bar. After several hours, I told them I was going to walk home and did so. I remember getting a good spanking for walking home that night. No matter where I went, I had to take my brothers and sister with me. I know now that I am very angry with my parents for all the drinking they did. I knew that there was no way I was going to drink or fight with my husband. I knew that I was trying to have everyone be happy. I worked as hard as I could to keep everything going smooth.

There was some abuse during those years, too. One day when I was twelve or so, we were out camping. I was going to change and go swimming. Just before I got my suit on, my mother said, "Come here and let your dad see how you are growing up." I felt funny and real, real embarrassed. To this day, I have a hard time looking at my body.

There could have been more abuse during those years until I was seventeen, but I have a hard time remembering. I have to really work at remembering the small events after I was seventeen.

My mother committed suicide when I was a junior in high school. Boy oh boy, talk about feelings bouncing off the walls. I blamed myself for her death. I was also very angry at her for leaving me. I really miss not being able to have her for a friend, someone to talk to, to share my happy times, like when I got married or when I had my children. I know now that I buried my feelings after I heard someone say, "Put it behind you. There is always someone worse off than you." So I didn't allow myself to go through the process of losing a loved one, or the feelings about the suicide itself.

My dad tried, I guess, to work out some of his feelings his own way. In the meantime, he was spending a lot more time at the bar. I had a feeling we kids were not important.

Now we are attending a couples therapy group. I'm now 43 years old, and with the help of the group, I'm able to learn how to accept the feelings I had growing up, and to deal with them in a healthy way.

When I was asked how I felt about my husband's molesting, at first I couldn't answer. I was so confused about it all. How could something this wrong be happening in my perfect world?

I had a hard time accepting the fact that it all wasn't my fault. There were several things I thought that if I had done different he would not have molested. I know now I am not to blame.

With my husband's help, I'm dealing with hidden memories and feelings as they surface: hurt, anger, pain, shame, being a bad girl.

It seems as time goes on and we work together and I don't keep pushing away my feelings and memories, I will find my mind a little lighter. I'm truly blessed with a partner who is learning more about himself and sharing that with me. He is also learning to listen to me and to help me.

Sometimes it is hard for me to face the fact that I have to take care of me first before I can really help take care of anyone else.

I know one thing for sure is there is always someone who will listen if I really want to be heard. I have to care enough about myself to reach out and talk about my feelings.

Many more memories are there to be looked at and feelings are there to be handled, but I know now that I have the support that I need to do it.

Thanks to my husband, my therapist, and my support group, I always have someone to turn to. Thanks for a new beginning. I will always be grateful.

Tunnel Of Untouchableness

Part I

January 1984. The morning recess was over. The children had settled back into their work and the classroom was very quiet. One child was reading aloud at the reading circle. The others around the table were concentrating on every word.

Suddenly, the school secretary paged me over the intercom, "Mrs. Jackson, would you come to the office and take a telephone call?" I remember feeling annoyed at the interruption. I was uncomfortable about leaving my class of first graders unsupervised while I ran over to the office and talked on the telephone.

I was standing in the entryway of the school with the school secretary watching and listening as I picked up that receiver to hear an alarming and confusing message. The woman identified herself as a social worker and told me that Sheila, my teenage daughter, was in her office. She assured me that Sheila was fine. The congenial tone of her voice convinced me that all was well. Then why was Sheila there? The social worker asked me to come immediately to her office. I was frightened, confused, and upset because I couldn't just walk out and leave my class. The secretary assured me that I could go and she'd cover for me. Was she listening to all this? So I grabbed my purse and drove downtown. Sheila must be pregnant, I decided on the way. Ah, I can handle this, I thought. I can be supportive and understanding.

The social worker greeted me and led me to her office. Sheila, I remember, looked stiff and uncomfortable. I wanted to burst out that everything would be all right. I felt so awkward and unnatural with the social worker there with her own agenda, so I said nothing. I could tell, even as Sheila spoke, that the words were rehearsed. Somehow that made the message and the situation even more unreal. Sheila said, "Daddy has been sexually molesting me." Immediately I felt like I was falling backwards. The rushing wind tunnel around me isolated me from feeling anything. I was so detached. I just wanted to get out of that airless, windowless cubbyhole of a room back into the sunshine. I must get back to school, I thought.

Rita, the social worker, said with disbelief, "Don't you want to hug Sheila?" I didn't really, but I did hug her. I remember how Rita and Sheila watched me, waiting for the truth to penetrate my barrier. It must have been unnerving to see a mother so apparently unmoved by the disclosure. I realized at the time that I was behaving strangely, but I was suddenly hollow without any emotion whatsoever. In time, the feelings and emotions would return to overwhelm and depress me beyond belief; but for the time, I was in my own tunnel of untouchableness. Sheila walked me to my car. Without a backward glance, I hurried back to school.

When I arrived at school, everything was completely normal, except I was viewing it from a long distance away. I remember suddenly thinking that my husband, Frank, might grab Joe, my two-year-old son, and head for the hills. I made a panicky call to his daycare center and told them that I was the only one that could pick up Joe today, not Frank. I wondered what he thought. He didn't ask, although he laughed an uncomfortable little laugh. Then I felt a rush of protectiveness towards Frank. He was my husband and he was in deep trouble. Could I help? I didn't think I could see him just then. I called his brother and told him, haltingly, that Frank was in trouble. He was with the county attorney and to please look out for him.

It was lunchtime, and my class was in the lunchroom. We had a potluck salad luncheon that day. The shadow of me walked into the faculty lounge and took my waldorf salad out of the refrigerator. I started dicing apples into the bowl, and then turned away. Someone will finish this, I thought. I need to be alone.

Just then the secretary told me that Frank was on the line. I didn't want to talk to him, but how could I refuse? So I answered his call. He said, "I'm surprised you'd talk to me," but he wasn't really. I believed that I should, in fairness to him, ask him if he'd molested Sheila, although I never for one moment doubted Sheila's word. He said, "Yes, I did." He also mentioned how he had never expected to be charged with sexual abuse, even when the county attorney called him unexpectedly into his office.

I remember feeling surprised that such an alarming request wouldn't trigger some guilt feelings. Frank had already outlined a series of actions for me to do to make sure he didn't go to jail. Could I get the afternoon off, he wondered. So I told the secretary I had a family emergency. Since the principal was out of the building for the day, she arranged for a substitute.

The rest of that day is rather a blur. I do remember sitting in a restaurant with Frank and looking at him with new eyes. I went to the phone booth there and called the social worker as I had promised earlier. She was genuinely concerned about me and wanted to know how I was doing. "Fine, fine," I said. "I'll be all right." I couldn't bear to hear the sympathy in her voice. For the first time that day, her interest was cracking through the walls of my protective tunnel. I could feel jolts of pain right through my body which left me weak and shaking. My face and throat were stiff and constricted with the efforts of not crying. My voice sounded squeaky as I forced the words out, "I'll be all right."

I remember talking with two attorneys that day. I felt debased to be pleading for Frank. I was relieved when it sounded like he wouldn't go to jail. Frank signed a deferred prosecution agreement and pledged to enter a treatment program at the mental health center for sexual offenders.

Sitting on our bed at home, I remember watching Frank pack a suitcase. Even though Sheila was staying with a friend for the weekend, I wanted him out of the house that night. I desperately needed the time and privacy to weep.

So ended the day that I awoke from dreaming, the day that ushered in reality with pain and heart-wrenching clarity. My new life was beginning. I was taking the first hesitant steps on my journey. I so wish I had known that day that my life was indeed changing, painfully, for the better. All I felt then was destruction, sadness so profound I could scarcely shed a tear, and a grieving for the losses of my marriage, my relationship with my beloved daughter, my family, and my faith in the goodness of life.

Part II

I've spent most of my life feeling isolated from my surroundings, especially from the people I have loved. I think this theme runs like a strand in and out through the years and events of my life. It explains my motivations and reveals my forbearance.

I was a very imaginative child who learned to create a private world where I felt a sense of belonging. I grew up by the Pacific Ocean and felt a kinship with the lonely stretches of beach. As an adopted child, I felt abandoned, different, and isolated from other people. When I was seven, my father died from a rare illness which he contracted from a tainted inoculation. In my family, we didn't cry or talk about Daddy's death, so I pretended that Daddy was away ''on location'' for his studio for months after he died. I developed bronchial asthma that year. I had a recurring nightmare where I found my father lying dead from a gunshot wound in his head, his rifle in his outstretched hand. I never spoke of the nightmare that I dreamed again and again during the years of my childhood. In my family, we kept our feelings and fears hidden.

I remember that I lied all the time as a child. I never understood why because the lies were meaningless. They never protected me nor glorified me. I once lied and said that my birthday was February 28 instead of February 27. I suppose I remember because my friend's mother corrected me.

I was a good student and earned a special place in the affections of my teachers. I was curious, interested, and loved learning. I always believed that I would someday be a teacher. College was my idea of heaven. I loved the heady atmosphere, the debates and discussions, the idealism, and the sense of belonging to an intellectual community.

Midway through college, I met and fell in love with a beautiful man. Jack was tall and slender, sensitive, creative, and extremely bright. He had a luminescent soul. I remember my first glance at him. He was standing at the stove and stirring with a long-handled spoon. His jeans were inches too short. As we were introduced, he turned towards me. I looked deeply into his eyes and my entire life changed. Jack lived with Jim in a rustic cabin in the coastal forests of California.

That night, we dressed in bed sheets, toga-fashion. We put wild flowers in our hair and walked through the darkness to a friend's steambath. I remember how exhilarating it was to emerge from the close, hot dampness into the starry night. Someone grabbed a hose and playfully sprayed us all. The water splashed our hot bodies with a hissing steam. We romped and laughed unselfconsciously. Then we lay exhausted and languid, side by side, and talked until morning.

Nearby San Francisco was filled with idealistic, charming dreamers in those days. The flower children were rebelling against materialism, loneliness, isolation, and self-interest. The hippie age was just beginning, and I had at last found my belonging place.

By the time Jack told me he was homosexual, we were deeply in love and committed to each other. I remember the night so well. By then Jack had moved to San Francisco. Standing naked by the window, he was silhouetted against the city lights as he turned and lit a cigarette. Then from across the room, he told me the truth about his homosexuality. I wrapped my arms around myself and tried to keep my heart from breaking. Then I dressed, left the apartment, and walked the streets of that beautiful city until the sky was light. I felt so inadequate and forlorn. I was still a virgin and in love with a man that didn't want me.

Jack stayed involved in my life for five more years. During that time, I became sexually involved with several men. Whether I was attempting to prove my attractiveness or in a twisted way to supplement my love relationship with Jack, I don't know. I became pregnant.

I had applied and been accepted into an academic exchange program for that fall. So two months pregnant, I was en route to Vienna, Austria for my junior year in college. Naively, I assumed everything would work out. In the meantime, I didn't want to miss an opportunity to study abroad.

My semester in Vienna was a wonderful, enriching experience. I plunged into the European lifestyle with enthusiasm. Naturally, my pregnancy couldn't remain hidden for long. I went through an extremely difficult time dealing with my mother and convincing her that I couldn't possibly put my baby up for adoption. I was wildly happy about the baby. I felt so connected to life. I knew in my heart that I would be a wonderful mother. I was filled with love for her, long before Sheila was born. My beloved Jack spent a great deal of time with me during my banishment to a home for unwed mothers. In a way, the baby belonged to us.

After Sheila's birth, I returned to school. I applied myself and completed the last two years of college in a year and a half. I also earned my fifth year and teaching credential. Jack remained my steadfast friend.

It was at this time in my life that I met Frank. Sheila was four years old. I was substitute teaching in Northern California. Frank had sky blue eyes—clear and honest and uncomplicated, it seemed to me. I was tired of loving Jack from afar, tired of being strong and independent. Along came a conservative man from an entirely different background, as far removed from the morass where I was stuck as possible. I grabbed at a chance for a conventional life. I fooled myself that I was in love with Frank. I didn't really know him.

I have always felt that I owe Frank a debt for rescuing me from the unhappy situation I was in. Consequently, I've put up with far more abuse than anyone deserves.

Our life together was a series of disappointments. Frank was an alcoholic. He became angry, argumentative, profane, unpredictable, and frightening when drunk. He was drunk almost every night of our marriage.

Frank was furious with me. Somehow, no matter how hard I tried, I never pleased him. He withheld his approval and love in a way that seemed punishing to me. I retreated more and more into myself. I sought validation through my work and was very dedicated to my teaching. Our relationship was extremely poor, but I fooled myself that no one else knew or was affected. Frank refused to have sex with me for months at a time and ridiculed me in countless small, personal ways. I was miserable and trapped by guilt and a sense of loyalty.

I remember so well how thrilled I was when after nine years of marriage, I was finally pregnant. When I shared this exciting and totally unexpected news with Frank, he responded, "Who's the father?" I was shocked and hurt beyond measure. He never had a single reason to doubt my fidelity, and he had to know that. Why was he tormenting me?

For the first six months of my pregnancy, he continued to question me. When I would cry, he'd laugh and say he was kidding. I felt desperately alone, disillusioned, and oh, so vulnerable. Frank begrudgingly attended a few childbirth classes.

From the day that I told him I was pregnant, Frank refused to make love with me. Even a year and a half after the baby was born, he still gave me excuses. He had a dozen reasons why I wasn't attractive to him. I was hurt and shamed by his rejections every time I would approach him. Sexual intimacy has always been very easy and natural for me. I was being destroyed by Frank's lack of interest. He could barely bring himself to touch me.

He bought me an outdoor lounge chair that summer when I was so big and uncomfortable. I was pathetically grateful for his kindness. Once, we stayed awake all night, laid on the couch together and watched a wonderful old movie. It makes me sad now to remember how happy I was to share something with him. Mostly, he went fishing and avoided being home.

As I lay in the hospital after my son was born, I felt so sad and alone. Frank called his parents to tell them of Joe's arrival. Then he went home. I tried to call my mother, but she wasn't home. I felt so empty.

I would have felt even worse if I had known what happened that day. Frank took Sheila out to dinner at his very good friend's house. They barbecued steaks, smoked Havana cigars, and drank Jim Beam whiskey. Unbeknownst to me, this had been going on for several years. Afterward, when Sheila and Frank went home, Frank molested Sheila. Somehow it's extremely hard to think that Frank could betray us all so vilely on the day his son was born.

The next day, Sheila came to the hospital to meet her brother. She stood outside the nursery window and sobbed. You see, Sheila had decided that she would have to tell me about the molesting if I had a girl baby. Because the baby was a boy, Sheila believed he was safe from Daddy. She wouldn't tell just to spare herself. She could handle it. I didn't understand her tears. I held her and reassured her that I'd never love her less, that she was my own special daughter. Sheila was thirteen years old that day. She carried such a burden of guilt and sadness. She kept her terrible secret to protect her new brother and her mother. Oh, how I wish I could relive that day and change the outcome of that conversation. Instead, Sheila lived in a secret world for two more years, where the reality of her unnatural incestuous relationship with her father overshadowed her daily life. How could I have so failed my daughter, I wonder? I saw none of the signs of the molesting, nor did Sheila have the trust to confide in me.

Part III

June 1988. It has been four and a half years since Sheila told me her father was molesting her. It's difficult to look back upon that time of my life, and painful.

I dreamed about Frank last night. I cradled his head in my lap, loved him, and laughed merrily at something he said. The dream stayed with me all day today, filling me with sadness and regret. Actually, Frank was never really like the man in my dream. . . .

A few days after Sheila told me about the sexual abuse, I received a phone call at school from Teresa. Teresa was the therapist recommended by the social worker. I remember agreeing that Sheila needed help dealing with the trauma. Teresa wanted me to seek help, too. I remember how awkward the conversation was. I was surprised by the hostility I heard in Teresa's voice. "Oh, no, you have just gotten off to a bad start with her," I told myself. "It will be much better when you meet."

At the mental health clinic, Sheila and I filled out a questionnaire with questions like: 1) Do you have trouble sleeping? 2) Have you gained or lost weight recently? 3) Do you often feel sad? 4) Are you having trouble remembering things? and more. We both filled out our forms, and nervously sat in the waiting room. Teresa introduced herself, and motioned for us to come.

I liked the look of Teresa. She had a hausfrau appearance—a round face, braided hair wrapped tightly around her head, and a full, dirndl type dress. She obviously liked Sheila. As I followed her up the stairs, I reiterated to myself that everything would be all right.

However, every answer I gave infuriated her. Teresa's anger confused me. She wanted me to list a problem I had on a piece of paper. I wrote down that I didn't like the way I would procrastinate. Teresa was looking for an issue relating to the abuse. I see that now. However, at the time, I couldn't look at the sexual abuse, or my relationship with Frank and Sheila. It was too new, too unbelievable, too painful.

I was used to people liking me and it was clear Teresa did not. She excused Sheila from the room and began yelling at me. I'm not sure of everything she said, but I do remember she claimed I knew Sheila was being molested. "No!" She said Sheila would grow to hate me in the course of this therapy. "No, no!" I was to blame. Didn't I know what was wrong when Sheila had ulcers? "I took her to the doctor!" In some states, the mother would face criminal charges automatically!

The Wall was in place. Sheila had the support of the social workers, Teresa, and the system on her side of The Wall. I was alone. I wanted to be on the team to cheer Sheila on! Instead, I was one of her enemies. Already I felt so guilty because I failed to see that Frank was molesting Sheila. Teresa's accusations further isolated me from Sheila and caused me to become distrustful and defensive. Was Teresa truly helping Sheila, I wondered again and again during the months that followed.

Teresa did say she had trouble relating to a mother's position because she hadn't dealt with her own feelings of betrayal stemming from the time she was gang raped. Why was she telling me this, I wondered during our first confrontation. Sheila and I polarized during the time she saw Teresa. Fortunately, Teresa moved to another city. Laurie became Sheila's therapist.

I tried to support both Sheila and Frank. I felt torn between them. Sheila seemed to reject me. Frank seemed to rely on me. I would meet Frank at the Country Kitchen for coffee, and we would talk for hours. He was my only friend—the only one I could talk to about my feelings. I needed to know about the abuse, and I couldn't trust anyone with my dreadful secret. I would ask Frank questions and hear little by little what had happened. I had to deal with the sexual abuse in small doses.

I couldn't talk to my therapist, Bruce. I didn't respect him or trust him. He was the kind of guy that never did his homework. Bruce would make assignments and forget about them. One week he'd contradict the very things he had said the week before, and then he'd cover his tracks by saying it was a test for me. He never seemed to care very much. Why didn't I change therapists? I wasn't thinking clearly, and it didn't dawn on me to fight for me.

During this period (which lasted from February 1984 to March 1985), I was acting irrationally. While driving, I would pull off to the side of the road and wonder where I was going. At other times, I would drive aimlessly through the streets and cry and cry. Then I'd return home as if nothing were wrong. I would arrive at school, and turn off my problems just like turning a switch. I'm sure no one realized the trauma I was going through. I remember stopping my car during a snow storm and wishing I could just die. It seemed so peaceful and quiet inside the cold car. I was in such pain. During those years, I stopped cooking meals. We ate cold cereal and sandwiches a lot. I couldn't sleep very well. In fact, I left the television in my bedroom on all night. I had no family to turn to for support. My mother was in a nursing home. My father had died when I was seven years old.

In March 1985, I made a phone call. I didn't realize at the time what an important call it would be! I called Sandi Ashley, and asked about a group that was forming for the wives of child molesters. Frank told me about the group, and urged me to call. He said it would help him "get out of the program" if I'd participate in the wives' group.

Sandi was straight-forward and friendly on the phone. She explained the group's purpose and invited me to come. I was so nervous that very first night. I wore one of Sheila's sweaters as a good luck omen. I could barely breathe by the time I walked down the long corridor. I paused by the door. "Are you Donna Jackson?" someone asked. Then several women laughed, and I almost turned and fled. There was some explanation given for their laughter—some mix-up of names and faces.

Soon the small room was filled with women. I'm not sure what I expected, but I remember being surprised by how "ordinary" and "regular" everyone seemed to be. That was reassuring. Sandi or Candy, the other therapist, opened the group that first night with a caution that it would take several meetings before we would feel comfortable with each other and be willing to share our feelings. Barely were the words spoken before there was a great outpouring of stories and feelings. Each woman, like myself, had been so isolated and alone that our need was overwhelming to share our stories and our feelings. We paired up and introduced our partners. At last we could reveal our anguish.

Judy suggested coffee afterwards to several of the women. Four of us met that night at a coffee shop, and the talk continued. This informal time after group became especially important to me. I had difficulty talking in the group. My problems seemed less urgent than others, and I didn't want to lose control and cry in group. I could share my story to the others over coffee. We became quite close.

Later, I began marriage therapy with Frank. Sandi became my therapist, and she also participated in those grueling sessions with Frank and Bruce.

I was shocked at Frank's attitudes and responses during therapy. With pressure applied to him, he responded in an exaggerated fashion, like a cartoon character. Sandi would raise her voice and say, "Bullshit, Frank!" in response to some outlandish thing he said. Frank would then turn in his chair and explode with anger at me! He couldn't confront Sandi and blamed me for his inadequacies. Bruce would ask Frank a question, and Frank would say, "This is supposed to be marriage therapy! Why are you picking on me? I don't have all the problems! Ask her. She's not perfect!" Bruce would remind Frank, "But you are the child molester!" and Frank would answer, "But I love my family. I want my family back together! I want my wife to be there for me."

In fact, Frank rarely called me by my name. I was either "wife" or "mother." It gave me a hollow feeling to realize I was just filling a role. I was not a person in my own right. I only existed as an appendage to him! Sandi said yes, it was true. If he could find someone else to fill his needs, he wouldn't even miss me.

After each session, I felt exhausted. The therapy turned on my mental light bulb and I could see. Suddenly I could see how Frank mistreated me. During the years, Frank had convinced me that he was always right. If I didn't agree, I was wrong. Frank's reality was crazy, but little by little, I lost sight of that. I believed I was the crazy one.

Also, I began to care about me and realize that I had a right to a life. Not happiness, quite. At that time, I didn't believe I'd ever be happy again, but I was rediscovering myself. It was as if I had been asleep for years, and suddenly I was awake. Why had I lost myself, I wondered? I knew what I wanted. Suddenly and without any doubts, I knew. I wanted a divorce so I could be me again. At the same time, I realized that there was no other choice if I considered Sheila's best interests. There was no way she could ever re-establish a relationship with Frank, and why should she be expected to? She deserved a mother at the very least. Everything fell into place all at once after months of being in a state of limbo. Joe would also be better off with a mother who could be honest with herself and respect herself. I was filled with strength and courage. I told the group that I had at last found the answer to my search. Then I told Frank. It was difficult to face him and say our marriage was over. We walked along the road in front of his house. He laughed in disbelief.

In the months following, we were divorced. Frank was only occasionally unpleasant. For the most part, he was cooperative. I expected more anger from Frank. I felt almost deflated by his lack of emotional involvement. Sandi reminded me that he was childlike in his emotional development. He was incapable of deep feelings.

Frank is very involved with Parents Without Partners. Once in a while, he tries to vent his anger and frustration to me over the phone. Frank sees Joe quite often. I worry about his influence with him. Frank calls Sheila, who is living in another town attending college. He still questions me about Sheila. "Will Sheila call me?" or "Will Sheila play tennis with me?" "Sheila won't come to the phone when I call." In frustration, he declares, "I won't call Sheila again. She'll just have to call me!" So I'm still forced to be in the middle. Frank knows how to manipulate me, and I sometimes fall into his trap. I still find myself trying to make everyone happy.

We have a beautiful little brick house, kind of like the third little pig's house in the nursery story. And yes, it's snug and cozy inside. And safe. Our home is filled with the good smells of cooking, the good sounds of laughter, and the good peace of happiness. Our wolf has come and gone.

Sheila finished her second year of college. She will be attending an academic exchange program in Europe next year. Joe will enter first grade this September. He is bright, creative, and extremely imaginative.

This is a story with a happy ending. Not quite a perfect ending though. Sheila has sexual problems, and continues to need therapy from time to time. I am not open enough with her, and I don't want to know more about her problems. I still have to force myself to hug Sheila. The ruins of The Wall remain. Joe has frightening nightmares. He uses anger to mask his feelings of hurt. Both of my children have difficulty showing their feelings, and saying no to their father. But we have all three survived our ordeal. I am the happiest I have ever been. I'm full of hope for the future.

Dads Don't Molest Kids They Love

All of my children were sexually molested by their father. I had a foster daughter for many years who was also molested by my ex-husband and my son. My son was physically and psychologically abused also.

I met Bill in 1960. I know he ran around with other women from the very beginning. Oftentimes, he chose very young girls. Bill was never very nice to me. If he bought me anything or took me anywhere, I had to pay for it with sex. He always told me I was fat and stupid, and how lucky I was to have him. I got so I really believed him. I thought I could never make it on my own because I wasn't smart enough. I was never able to have a close loving relationship with my two older children because Bill always told them I was a weak person and they had to shelter me. That way he could stop them from confiding in me. We are closer now. It has been difficult because the distance was there for so many years.

Bill always favored Peggy over Derek. It was real hard for me to understand why. He bought her a car when she was fifteen. Derek always had chores to do, like take care of the pigs or feed the calf. But Peggy didn't have to do anything. I would ask him why he didn't do things with Derek like take him fishing or hunting and he'd say, "He's too lazy to get out of bed," or "He's too stupid to know how to shoot a gun." It really broke my heart to see him treat Derek like crap and act like Peggy was a princess. So I found myself turning more to Derek, trying to do things with him. Then Bill would accuse me of not loving Peggy, which of course is not true. I love all of my children dearly and would fight anyone for them.

When I found out Bill molested them, I wanted to kill him. He never had treated us well. When Derek would try to hug Bill or kiss him good night, he'd say, "What's the matter with you? Are you queer?" He would knock himself out being Mr. Wonderful to the neighbors. He'd fix their cars or their kids' bikes, and lend them money. When he had rented trailer houses, he'd let people live there for months and not pay any rent. But I had to beg for money for food, or clothes for the kids. If I bought them toys, he would really raise hell.

He didn't work very often. He always was lazy. So I always worked while he stayed home with the kids. He really had no respect for any of us or for himself either.

He used to go to the bathroom and leave the door open, or shower and stand naked shaving with the door open. If I told him to close the door because I didn't think the children should be subjected to him exposing himself, he'd say, "You're just ashamed of your body."

I found out about the abuse when my youngest daughter, Jackie, was five. She told me her dad made her look at naughty pictures and take off her clothes and he would rub himself on her. He told her if she told me, he would spank her. I thank God every day she was brave enough to tell me. She said she was really tired of it and wanted me to make him stop.

When I asked him about it, he said she was lying. I told him I knew she wasn't, and if he ever touched my little girls again, I would kill him.

About six months before that, I caught my son in my foster daughter's bed. She was eight years old. I was devastated. I told Bill and he beat Derek real bad. I was foolish enough to think it never happened before and wouldn't happen again.

After Jackie told me about the abuse, I got a divorce as soon as I could, and the girls and I moved out. My older daughter was on her own. My son was having behavior problems. I couldn't handle him, so he stayed with his dad. I never told Peggy or Derek why I got a divorce. They thought it was because of Bill's girlfriends.

When Amanda, my foster daughter, was thirteen, she started running away. I found out that Derek had been molesting her for a long time. When I asked her why she didn't tell me, she said she didn't think I would believe her. Amanda was taken from our home and placed in a foster home. She had lived with us since she was two years old. I felt like someone tore my heart out.

Jackie, my youngest daughter was devastated. Especially when "they" came to get her things. I hated my son at that time. I could believe Bill would do a terrible thing like that, but not my son.

I called Peggy, and told her about Jackie and about Amanda. I didn't think she would believe me because she was always so close to her dad. When she didn't scream at me or call me a liar, I asked her if her dad ever did anything to her. She said yes. I asked what he did, and she said "everything." I asked when he started, and she said she couldn't remember, but that he quit when she was nine years old. I asked her why she didn't tell me. She said when she was little, she thought that was the way it was supposed to be. When she got older, she was afraid. He told her if she told me I would kill him and I would go to prison. Then she and Derek wouldn't have anyone to take care of them. If I had a gun at that time, I would have killed him.

Derek and Peggy seem to resent (especially Derek) Jackie and the things she has. I try to explain to him that I can do things for her that I was not allowed to do for them.

Bill had triple bypass surgery a year ago in April and was found dead in his camper at the lake in July. I can't honestly say that I am sorry he's dead.

Derek still has terrible nightmares about Bill chasing him with a chain saw. Peggy thinks he should have been father of the year. I can't understand how she can defend him after what he did to her and her brother and sisters. He tore our family apart. One day Peggy was talking about how wonderful he was, and Jackie said, "Dads don't molest kids they love." Peggy didn't say a word. She looked sick.

The other day Peggy and I were scuffling with each other and I said, "Be careful. I'm fragile." Peggy said, "Yeah, Dad always said he was afraid you'd break." I think the dirty bastard did everything he could to break me in every way possible. I also think my therapist helped me to live again and find out what it's like to be happy for the first time in many, many years.

Why Us?

"Mom, you'd better talk to Rebecca and find out what she meant." My son Peter said these words to me as we were on our way to pick up my husband from work.

Molested—that is what she meant—and Lloyd was the molester. Our adopted daughter, now a teenager, had been a victim of her father's sexual, physical, mental and emotional abuse.

"Why me?!?"

That was the first thought that I had. Looking back now, I feel real pain in realizing my first thought was not, "Why her?" She was a child. She was the victim. I believe today my cry really was, "Why us? What has happened in our lives and in our marriage that we came to this?" Our whole family has been victims of what happened: Rebecca, myself, our other children, and even Lloyd, the molester. In the past four and a half years, I have looked at many feelings and events in our lives. I realize that we were people in turmoil and pain for a long time. I believed, hoped, wanted us to be a family. We really were not.

The ideal family—that has been my goal for as long as I can remember, a family with a perfect mom, a loving, caring father, and happy, cherished sons and daughters.

It was my dream and it would come true, no matter what the cost to me. This impossible dream was buried so deeply inside of me that I was not aware of it, at least the impossible part of it. My family was not going to experience the hurt and separation that I felt my family of origin had suffered. My dad was a good man, a hard worker, an alcoholic. I have three sisters and two brothers. In sharing with two of my sisters, I find our memories differ greatly. I recall much hurt and sadness and some happiness and fun. One sister remembers very differently, one quite similarly. My memories are from outside, looking in.

I was raised by grandparents from age five until I married at 22, gentle, loving, caring people. There is a great deal of pain connected to not living with my mom and dad despite the good life I had with my grandparents. I always wondered why they didn't want me. I wondered what I had done between birth and five years old that was so terrible that I couldn't stay with my family. Maybe it was that I was just bad, period. Maybe I wasn't big enough or capable enough to help my mom. I think this last may have been reinforced by the fact that my mom took in a mid-teen girl to help her soon after I went to live with my grandparents. I wonder if this was the beginning of my need to take care of everyone and everything.

The adult part of me understands the reasons I lived with my grandparents. The child in me hurts and still asks, "Why?" I was just a little child and wanted my mommy. I have daughters and sons. I would die before I chose to give one of them away. In spite of understanding the circumstances, I feel I was given away. That hurts like hell.

My feeling of guilt is very deep. I was safe, cared for. My sisters and brothers in my memory and feelings were not. I cannot challenge any of their feelings or memories. Those belong to each of them and are valid for them. Mine belong to me and are valid for me.

So my children, our children, were going to be loved, cherished, protected, never hurt, never in pain. A very distorted idea of the reality of life. But we were going to be a "perfect" family. And this would happen because I could be the perfect wife and mother. I had to be perfect. In my mind and heart, if I was not perfect, I was a failure.

For years, I worked very hard at projecting that image to everyone, including my-self. We had a large family, nine in all, including the child who we were told "should be grateful that she was lucky enough to be adopted by you." In my determination to be perfect, I had convinced Lloyd to adopt a Third World orphan. We were heroes in my eyes, and, I hoped, in the eyes of our families and friends.

On the outside, we lived a life that everyone saw as a beautiful, caring Christian family. So many times, people said to me, "How do you do it? You have such a beau-tiful family." Yes, our children, each of them, are beautiful. They lived in a very dys-functional atmosphere. We projected a really great image. We worked very hard at the image. There were no problems in our marriage relationship, our family life, at least not any that Super Mom couldn't handle. If only I could take care of it, we'd all be happy.

There were good times, happy and fun times, special moments.

But underneath there was no solid foundation of mutual respect, care, love, under-standing or acceptance between Lloyd and me.

Deep within I knew this: There was something wrong. In my mind, it was my fault, my failure. For many reasons, I have had a difficult time believing that anyone else may be responsible if there are problems anywhere in my circle of life. In my marriage especially, I felt that all difficulty, stress, and pain was my fault. Lloyd told me so in direct and subtle ways. My family told me so, too. "He is such a good man. He tries so hard. You shouldn't feel that way." If everyone could see this was true, then the problems must be all my fault. Unfortunately, the problems I sensed were real.

So I tried all the ways that I knew, and all of the ways I searched to learn to change me. That way our marriage and family would really be perfect. I read books, went to workshops, talked to people, cried, yelled, prayed, and struggled to become perfect, so that we would all be okay.

When I reflect on my struggles and pain, I sometimes wonder why I am still here. I believe it is my deep faith in a God who loves me. The core belief was always inside, even though for many years, I did not realize it.

I felt so utterly worthless for many years. I tried very hard to be worthy, especially of Lloyd and his love. I had dinner ready when he was ready, his clothes washed and ironed when he needed them, and the house neat and clean when he came home. After nine kids and years of trying, I gave up on the house cleaning. I just couldn't care any longer. I would buy cards to tuck inside his lunchbox—sweet cards, loving cards, sexy cards, funny cards, cards for all occasions, any occasion, and no occasion—gifts, from me or from the kids on special days. This was part of my job as a good wife. The fact that he hardly ever remembered a special day made no difference. In my way of thinking and feeling, I wasn't good enough to be special to anyone.

"Do you know Lloyd is having an affair with Pam?"

Denial—total and complete. I believed him. I had to or all that perfection would be destroyed. A few months later on our way home from a meeting, I heard the truth. Yes, he had an affair, but it was over. Some of the time it had happened on the job. The pain of knowing he had had sex with someone else while telling me he loved me and thought our sexual life was great, tore my heart apart. I loved him and trusted him. I felt betrayed and worthless. Along with the pain came terror at what could have happened had they been discovered at work. Fired—no job, no wages. We could have lost our home. The shame of everyone knowing—although almost everyone but me knew already. Then came the guilt. If I had been a good wife, he never would have had to have an affair. Again, my fault, my failure.

During these years of guilt and pain, there were also deeply buried feelings of shame, rage, resentment and hurt. I knew no way to express my feelings in appropriate ways, to seek help, to grow, or to respond not react. If I could change all that happened as a result, I would do so now. All those feelings came out in a terrible, destructive way centered on Rebecca. I began and continued to abuse Rebecca, physically and emotionally. I beat her with my hand and a belt. I forced her to stand in a corner until she fell asleep because she was naughty. I forced her to sit at the dinner table until she fell asleep because she had failed to finish her meal. I used ugly, vicious words to wound her.

I am still not really, totally sure of why I used Rebecca to vent my anger and pain on. Perhaps I felt she wasn't really mine. I had not carried her within me, given birth to her, nursed her. Or maybe I knew that she would accept all the pain without fighting back or telling. Maybe these reasons, maybe others. I just don't know.

Rebecca was a perfect victim for Lloyd—quiet, compliant, terrified of him. I helped her become that victim.

Many times I asked Lloyd to discipline her because I was afraid of what I was doing to her. I thought she was safe with him. Then he would use his belt on her and I would tell him to stop. He was doing exactly what I did. I wanted that to stop. I wanted Lloyd to protect her from me. Instead, I gave him a child who had no protection at all. Her safety was lost.

There was no way she could tell me of the sexual abuse. Hadn't I let her dad hurt her? Her belief was, I am sad to say, that I knew about the sexual abuse. I either wanted it to happen or I just didn't care. I know she cannot believe me when I say I did not know, and if I had learned it was happening, I would have tried to stop it.

I asked Peter that night on the way to pick up Lloyd why he wanted me to talk to Rebecca. While I was away from home, an argument took place. Don, another son, said to Rebecca, "You shouldn't feel that way." Her reply was, "If what happened to me had happened to you, you'd feel this way, too." When I asked Rebecca what she meant, she told me, "Daddy touches me in places I don't want him to." I knew he had done it. Why I felt so sure, why the fear was immediate, I don't really know. Sexual abuse was the last thing I ever thought Lloyd would do.

The next day, I confronted Lloyd with Rebecca present. I asked her to tell me in front of him what she had told me the night before. She did. He said, "It's not true." I looked at Rebecca and asked her if it was true. The look on her face told me that she was going to say it was not true. Then I told her that for her sake, she had to say the truth, no matter what happened to Lloyd. If he had molested her, she must tell me. She did, "It's true." I told her to go back to her brothers and sisters. I said to Lloyd, "Well?" He did not say a word. He didn't have to. The look on his face said it all. I felt my world collapse.

Lloyd and I had been going to a counselor to help our marriage. What could help when there was no real honesty? I sent Rebecca to the counselor and lived in fear at what would happen when she disclosed the abuse.

One day Rebecca had been home only forty-five minutes from a session when two social workers came. She told the counselor of the abuse. The next few minutes were agony, especially for our two youngest children. They adored Rebecca. Having her leave hurt and scared them. I held them and tried to assure them it would all be okay. In my heart, I did not believe it ever would be okay again.

The next couple of months were confusion and fear. Visits from the social worker, a foster home for Rebecca, wondering what would happen to Lloyd and to all of us.

What did happen was a miracle, in fact, two of them: for Lloyd and me, the Sexual Assault Treatment Program; for myself and our children, a wonderful family therapist in our home town. Lloyd admitted to the sexual abuse and received a deferred prosecution. The main condition of his deferred prosecution was sex offender treatment.

I spoke of the miracle of coming to the Sexual Assault Treatment Program. Well, it was and is. At that time, it felt like a trap, like a persecution of Lloyd and me. Even though I knew Lloyd had molested, I was in denial about our whole life. My attitude was go down, play the game, get it done, and get out. I hated the therapists and the other men in Lloyd's group. All that I knew of the program was what Lloyd told me. Of course, his view of the program was not very accurate. All he wanted to do was get finished.

For a part of this time, I was in Sandi's group. I fought it all the way. I did like Sandi, but I felt she could not understand me or my feelings. In retrospect, I can see how very well she did understand me, but I did stop going to her group.

Then in my mind, this program that was going to help us began to "play dirty." Lloyd was just sitting on his butt, doing no real work at becoming healthy. I was still doing a great job of protecting and taking care of him. He was told he had to move out of the house. I was in a panic! What was I going to do? How could I manage on my own? The reality that I had been doing it all on my own for twenty years meant nothing to me. I felt I was not capable and was not strong; but I was and I am. It has taken a while to see and accept myself in those ways, but I get better at it each day.

Lloyd still had not chosen to do the real hard work he needed to do to get well. So for a time, there was no contact between him and our family. Then there was very limited contact between Lloyd and me. Slowly Lloyd began to realize he had to change. No one, not even me, could or would do it for him.

We were invited to become a part of the couples group for sex offenders and their wives. We were one of the first five couples.

Lloyd at last began to do his work. He disclosed that he had also sexually abused our oldest daughter Mandy and her friend Beth. Neither was subjected to the brutality that Rebecca received, but they are sexual abuse victims whose lives were harmed terribly by their treatment at Lloyd's hands.

Learning of Beth's abuse caused me a great deal of fear. I thought that her mother would press charges and Lloyd would go to prison. Because he was in treatment, she did not do so. Discovering Mandy's abuse hit me with another blow to my self-esteem. I did not realize that Lloyd could do this to a child that he fathered and watched come into the world. I did not protect her either. I did not know I had to protect any of my children from their dad.

Learning of Mandy's sexual abuse helped me to understand much of her early sexual activity. She became sexually active at about 14, became pregnant, and gave birth to her son in her 16th year. I was also more able to realize why she felt toward me as she did.

Rebecca moved out of state with her foster family about two years ago. She finished high school, has a job, and plans to further her education. I feel she has not received much needed therapy. After she left Montana, she was given the choice of going or not going, and she decided not to go. I hope that one day she will be able to find help and finish healing the harm that was done to her.

The couples group has been a safe haven for me. I can laugh, cry, grieve, rage, confront Lloyd, and be confronted. I am accepted and loved here. I am part of a real family.

There are many things that contribute to a molester's behavior: anger, fear, hate, blame, low self-esteem, alcohol, and drugs. It goes on and on. These are the same things that can influence someone like me to behave as I did. The bottom line, as hard as it is to admit, is that each of us chooses to do what we do. We also have the choice to change, to seek help, to work at becoming healthy, to grow. We have the choice to become the whole person we were created to be. Lloyd and I are making that choice. That is why we are in the Sexual Assault Treatment Program. That is why we are still married.

My faith teaches that after death, life is changed, not ended. I have come to believe that after molestation, disclosure, therapy, and hard work, life is changed, not ended.

Shadows That Haunt Me

In the beginning, my thoughts were: "This doesn't happen to people like us."

I am telling my story for the wife, the mother, who has gone or is going through the trauma of living with a child molester. I hope it will give you something to relate to. Sexual abuse is coming out of the woodwork. Yes, it happens. Incest happens to many children, leaving families scarred. Incest is demeaning and destructive to each member of the family. I want to share the trauma of sexual abuse in our family. My hopes are that by reading about our lives, experiences, feelings and frustrations, you who are victimized by the violence of sexual abuse will find that this book will be a source of strength and support, and you will feel less isolated from the world. I hope this story will help you to overcome this family tragedy and continue life to its fullest. Don't feel alone—because you're not.

What is marriage? What are the important qualities that make a marriage happy, meaningful, and make a marriage last? For me, trust was the important factor, total trust between husband and wife. It was the one thing I was working hard to accomplish, knew would happen someday. I told myself things were getting better. Really they were falling apart—our marriage, our family—each one of us was being destroyed.

My life was not happy anymore. I had no personal goals. Life now meant surviving any difficulties my husband, Richard, had incurred. This meant living around Richard's schedule; moving from town to town when necessary, which seemed to be often; isolating myself to avoid confrontations with people Richard had taken advantage of, and feeling empty inside, so very empty.

My hopes were high—my dreams are still there—but after years of being the supportive wife, the loving mother, my marriage was falling apart. I asked myself: "Is it my fault? What should I or shouldn't I have done?"

I am blessed with three healthy, bright children. I centered my life around them. I would be the best mother I could. I could certainly fulfill this goal, as I love children very much, especially my own. Nothing gave me more pleasure than to hear their laughter and see their exuberant faces.

Tammi, the oldest, is a tall blonde, blue-eyed, lanky fourteen-year-old. Tammi has always been my in-house comedian, with a quiet, reflective personality, always able to make me laugh when life seemed hopeless. Little did I know about the tears she wept silently, living in a secret world of fear and abuse by her stepfather that had been a way of life for several years. Until that Halloween night, I could never understand her spur-of-the-moment irrational behavior.

Terri, on the other hand, is the mild-mannered, easy-to-please middle child, who made an extra effort to comply with her father's every command. She also was in a secluded sexually abusive relationship with her father. Her childlike face shines when she's happy, but when she's sad, it reflects the empty, hurtful feelings deep inside her soul.

The youngest of my children is Richard, Jr.; our Richie, the baby of the family, and very much treated as such. We cherished our blond-haired, blue-eyed boy. He developed a very outgoing personality. The girls and I taught Richie far beyond his years. But as the years progressed and Richie got older, he became aware of the lack of attention and time his father had to offer him. Frustration was the emotion he felt when he was told to stay home, only to realize that Dad was taking one of the girls. Dad never had the time for him. No matter how much time Richie spent with his dad, he never got much out of the relationship. He's a very outgoing child, with much feeling for other people.

Richard—the husband, the offender, a very boisterous man, makes friends easily. He's always the life of the party. But at home, he's very self-centered. Everyone lives around his schedule. He's notorious for having his own way—or else.

Me—the mother and wife. Living in a trap. Not knowing how to get out. Feeling marriage is everlasting, and I will just have to endure a controlling husband. I will not reflect on myself as you will come to know me as the first person in telling this story. You will progress with me along a road of many emotions, some very hard to bear.

❋ ❋ ❋

One day it all came crashing down. I felt like the worst mother in the world. I was convinced certainly that was true.

Richard and I were on our way to school where Tammi is an eighth-grade student. She had been very hard to get along with lately. I found it especially hard to communicate with her. She never wanted to stay home, and was threatening to run away. In a futile attempt to avoid the worst, I made an appointment with her school counselor. We arrived on time for our meeting, but it just so happened he had a student in his office who had an emergency. After waiting about fifteen minutes, we went in.

As we were entering his office, I noticed our other daughter, Terri, a seventh grader, walking down the hall with a teacher, sobbing and hanging her head. I became quite concerned and questioned that something must be wrong. The counselor then suggested it was probably nothing serious, and we got on with our discussion about Tammi. The counselor reinforced our daughter's good character, sound moral standards, and said it was probably nothing more than the normal eighth-grade student problems. So we left feeling reassured, yet I was still concerned about seeing Terri so upset.

I remember Terri and Richie coming home from school that day. It was Halloween night, and we were preparing for trick or treaters. Then something strange happened. Terri came to me and said a lady would be calling me about 6:30 that evening. I asked her why, but she informed me that she was told not to discuss it with me until the lady called.

Strangely enough, this left her father pacing the floor, very concerned this may involve him, which only confused me more. Finally Richard insisted I must go in and ask Terri if this involved him. "Have I done something?" he asked. When I asked Terri this, she only looked at me and said, "You're going to be so hurt." I felt like everyone was playing a game with my mind. Nothing was making sense to me.

My husband was obviously very upset. For what reason, I could not imagine. My daughter was also very upset, staying in her room. I felt like her father's presence was threatening to her. I did not understand why.

It was 6:30. The tension had risen to an extremely high level by now. Finally the telephone rang. I went downstairs. Something inside told me to take this call in private. My stomach was already in knots as I answered the phone.

"Mrs. Miller? This is Janet L. from human services. I am a social worker. Do you know why I'm calling?" I answered, "No." She continued, "Terri went to the school counselor today and said her father has been fondling her. He in fact has been fondling both girls. I need to come out and talk with you and your husband tonight. When would be the best time?" There was no time for me to digest what this woman had just told me. I quickly answered with, "Come right away." She asked if the children and I would be all right until she arrived, and I assured her we would be fine.

I hung up the phone and tried to regroup. Did she really say fondling? Why would Richard do that to Terri, his own daughter? What should I do? All I could think was, "This doesn't happen to people like us."

I knew what to do. First I went upstairs into Terri's room, hugged her, and told her I was sorry, so very sorry. We cried together.

My next step was to confront Richard. I asked him as he sat slouched on the couch if he had indeed fondled the girls. His response was, "I never screwed the girls." His evading my question only quickened my anger. I responded with, "I did not ask you that. I said: Did you fondle the girls?'' His response was yes. I felt myself become physically ill at that moment. My thoughts flashed back to the conversation Richard and I had had three months ago. The subject of incest with stepchildren came up. I asked Richard, ''You would never do that, would you?'' ''Oh, no,'' he replied. ''I think that's disgusting.'' He was a true con artist. To vomit on Richard would not even begin to express how vile I felt his actions were.

As I waited for Janet to arrive, I continued with matters at hand, sending the children out to trick or treat, and giving candy to the ghosts and goblins lurking at our door. This night the demons were out—and the real demon was sitting in my living room. As he sat on the couch not able to look me in the eye, he stewed about going to jail. ''This is it,'' he said. ''It's over now. I'll be going to jail.'' I heard no concern for the girls, only what would happen to him.

The social worker came, and the three of us sat at the table. She confronted Richard with the things the girls had said. Both Tammi and Terri were victims, neither one aware that the other one was being molested until this day. He sat with his face in his hands, not looking at anyone.

It was Janet's suggestion that the girls stay at a friend's house for the night. I could not imagine having the girls away from me. Why should they have to leave the home? They did nothing wrong. At my suggestion, Richard went to a friend's house to stay, and the girls stayed home with Richie and me.

Richie went to bed fairly early, exhausted from trick or treating. He was not aware of the problems, as we had covered up why Richard was gone.

The girls and I sat up for quite a while and talked. We found it uncomfortable to talk much about the molestation. We were all uneasy with what would take place now. We all needed to sleep, but found it to be a restless night.

The next day, there were several things to do. First on the agenda was to go to the mental health center and talk to a psychologist. We were very fortunate to get Jim, who has been very helpful to us.

After this, we visited the social worker to make videotapes of the girls' story. Janet being a very calm, soothing person, is easy to talk to. She has a caring quality in her professionalism. She took the girls one at a time into a room with all the video equipment set up. Then she taped the ugly details of what took place during the molesting.

I found myself to be extremely exhausted as one then the other went with Janet. Several times, Janet questioned my stability. I felt my whole self being drained.

After the videos were made, Janet asked if I wanted to see them. I had mixed emotions. As a wife, I didn't want to know. But there was a stronger part of me. I had to know exactly what their father had done to better understand the trauma my daughters were going through. This is the only way I could help them now. They had to know I was beside them, supporting them, and most important, believing them one hundred percent.

Janet, the girls and I went into the video room. First we viewed Tammi's. We all watched as Tammi described what her father did. As Terri's video came on, she asked to leave the room. Tammi and I stayed and viewed Terri's video. I felt very sad for my daughters. We sat in Janet's office for some time after we saw the videos until we felt strong enough to leave and go home.

Richard was still staying with a friend, and the weekend was approaching. I had assured Richard the girls and I wanted him to get help. We didn't want to punish him, only wanted him to get better. I feared for his life that weekend. He seemed so very unstable. I drove back and forth that weekend—to reassure Richard I wasn't deserting him, and to make sure he didn't make an irrational decision—and to be at home to support the girls and take care of Richie. This was an extremely difficult time for me. I had not begun to deal with my own emotions, but felt it necessary to stand in the middle and be strong for both sides.

First thing Monday morning, Richard called his attorney, as we knew the county attorney would be notified by Human Services.

Richard then informed me he had rights, too. He had to defend himself. I wasn't sure what he meant by that. At this point, I felt it necessary to make sure Richard knew where I stood. I said to Richard, "If you are going to deny these charges, we will go to court, and the girls will tell their story. I would hope you wouldn't put them through that. But I believe them. The facts are there. I'm backing them one hundred percent."

After talking with his attorney, he assured me he didn't want to put the girls through a court trial. The county attorney made a deal with Richard. He would get a deferred prosecution if he went through a sex offenders treatment program at the mental health center, a two-year program of extensive treatment. It was to Richard's benefit to accept the deal. It was also a great relief to the girls because there would be no court appearance, no arrest, and ultimately nothing would appear in the local newspapers.

The next week began, and I did not know what to tell Richie about Dad's absence. Jim suggested being honest with Richie, and telling him why his dad had to leave. We had no idea of the duration of Richard's absence from the home. At first, we all thought about one week. Then as we got involved with counseling, and Richard was going through the evaluation for the sex offender program, we realized it would be a while before he came home. One requirement of the sex offender program is for the offender to move away from home. Also as time went on, I realized the importance of Richard being away. The girls felt much safer when he was not around. I was the parent the girls felt safe with.

As the months wore by, Richard moved from place to place, leaving delinquent debts behind. Holding a job was impossible for him.

Sunday was family day—Richard's day to visit us and spend the day. This felt so unnatural. I didn't like having him around, watching every move we made. It knots my stomach this very minute thinking about it. After a few months of Sunday visits, family counseling, marriage counseling, and individual counseling, Terri said she felt like her father was grooming her, and didn't want to see him or be around him.

This only added to everyone's frustration. Marriage counseling was not working. Richard was not doing well in group therapy, and family therapy was getting us nowhere. Everyone was too frightened of Richard. Yet no rifts were made. Everyone played the game they knew so well. Keep Dad happy. Making Dad angry at you only caused you grief, usually for what seemed an eternity, if only for a few days.

I had started a new job only days after discovering the incest. It was very difficult working an eight-hour day, raising my children alone, and supporting everybody emotionally. Richie had pneumonia. The girls were diagnosed as having mononucleosis. I felt overwhelmed. I found myself crying on the job, not knowing if I should stay home with sick children and be a good mother or if I should go to work to be a good provider. I couldn't cope. I had to do both. Richie would ask me to stay home with him. I would leave for work and cry for the whole fifteen-mile drive, wondering if my four-dollar-an-hour job was worth keeping, or if I should ask for help and be home with my children this summer.

After various episodes of anger—Richie trying to run away, throwing a new pair of eyeglasses in the farmer's field, never to be found again—my answer came one day at work. I met with the office manager, and we mutually agreed I needed to be home with my children, for their mental health as well as my own. After a few days my job ended, and I became a full-time mother receiving welfare.

When I was growing up, my own family never received welfare. I only thought of very poor people using food stamps, although during my marriage to Richard we depended on them for food in between jobs. From May 1985 to September 16, 1985, I was home with my children. Even though I hated using food stamps to buy food, it was a wise choice I had made. We grew a lot that summer — afternoons at the lake, picnics. That has probably been our best summer, the summer of 1985.

With summer coming to an end, it was clear I had to address my relationship with Richard. I couldn't continue living this way. It seemed too dangerous. So I made an appointment at the mental health center.

It took months of work with my counselor, Jim, to prepare myself to meet with Richard. I had to be well-organized and straight to the point. I didn't want to be emotional or fearful. I prepared everything I needed to say in writing, then reviewed it with Jim.

Finally it was ready—time to tell Richard. Fear was everywhere. I could not predict what Richard's reaction would be. I had no idea what to expect. I couldn't eat, sleep, or think straight. I woke up that morning upset. My former boss had been a very positive influence for me during this time in my life, so I shared with him what was to come. He reassured me I could do it. All would go well. The feeling I experienced deep in my stomach cannot be described. It's almost like another part of me that only hurts that way, like someone is stabbing me and turning a butcher knife under my diaphragm. I can see an arm and hand holding a black-handled butcher's knife, turning the knife in my gut, letting go, only to grip it again, and turn and turn and turn. That is the pain and fear I felt inside me. This is what I wrote and read to Richard at a meeting with each of our counselors present:

"Ten months have passed since the molesting became known. During that time until July, you continued to write NSF checks, resulting in being irresponsible with your money, causing many more debts, which in turn hurts me and the children. Because of your irresponsibility with money, you are unable to help support us.

"You have continued to lie to us until I find things out and confront you with it. Then and only then do you admit it.

"On numerous occasions I have asked you to level with me—give me an honest answer. Total honesty is the only communication I will respond to in the future. I will verify the story as often as I feel necessary, and with whoever need be.

"I will not confront and discuss major issues with you, except with your or my counselor at mental health.

"I feel the sexual molesting of the girls to be the most destructive behavior you have had. But we must realize that only stopped because of the girls. In no way did you contribute to the sexual abuse stopping.

"Now because of extreme measures that have been taken, the sexual abuse has ended. But this leaves other negative parts of your behavior still there.

"The lying and having all of your material wants met, no matter what the cost, is still going on. You are still deceiving us whenever you want to.

"I am not willing to continue our relationship this way. I have already found legal counsel, and am seriously contemplating divorce. I am willing to wait a period of three months, until December 1st, to move in that direction. There are no guarantees that I won't file for divorce. I am feeling strongly pulled in that direction now. But I don't want to make a hasty decision, and feel I should give it some more time.

"Our marriage cannot be worked on at this time. Individual therapy is needed now. I feel that is a priority. If in the future we are able to work our own individual problems out, then we can consider counseling together. Time will be the determining factor in that situation.

"We are not dealing with a problem that is only one problem. We are dealing with a very complex problem, having many areas to work on. I feel we need to work on our own weaknesses at this point.

"I will support you, Richard, when you are doing the things you are supposed to do, when you are honest to yourself and to others. I cannot support you when you don't do the things you should to help yourself change.

"I cannot be your strength. You must be your own source of strength, just as I am for myself. I cannot keep you in the program or kick you out. Only you can do that. The sex offender program is for you. I suggest you make the most of it. You have the opportunity to change your life for the better, but only you can make that happen. I truly hope you do, as over the years, I have seen many good and caring qualities in you.

"I also know that I cannot change you. You must change yourself — for your-self—not for me.

"We will still need to keep in touch to some degree because there are financial matters to discuss and work out. Also you have an obligation to help in certain areas, such as: Repairs on the house; financial support; repairs on the car (when you are work-ing). I cannot afford to hire someone to do these things.

"These are positive changes in your behavior I feel should be worked on consis-tently and in depth, starting now:

1. No more lying to anyone. If there is anything else hidden from me or lied to me about, I want to know now and not find out from someone else later. This will only add to my reasons for getting a divorce.
2. No more writing bad checks.
3. No spending money needlessly on yourself. The only money you should be spending for yourself is to take care of your needs, such as shelter, food, clothing, therapy bills. Leftover money can be used for past debts and support of your family."

That was August 29, 1985. It kept getting worse. The truth was a lie, and a lie the truth. There was no distinguishing them one from the other. Richard was not to be trusted, believed, or even liked as far as I was concerned. I had my fill. My sympathy for him was gone. I was hating the man that had taken up more than fifteen years of my life—my sanity, my hope, my happiness. I had a right to hate him.

On September 25, 1985, I had another meeting at the mental health center with my counselor, Richard and his counselor. This time I told Richard that I couldn't wait any longer, and I was proceeding with filing for divorce immediately. The meeting went like this, with me speaking to Richard. Again I wrote my thoughts out on paper:

"I have decided to proceed with the divorce now because:

1. I don't love you.
2. I don't want to continue in this marriage. I don't see any future for this marriage.
3. I don't see any possibility of recapturing my feelings for you, even if you do change.
4. The sexual molestation of the girls is the deciding issue for ending our marriage. I feel I can forgive you for what you have done; but this does not make it possible for me to love you again ever.

"I hope we can remain friends, mostly for Richie's sake. I want to make this as easy on Richie as I possibly can. I know this will be difficult for him. How we deal with this in respect to Richie will determine how well he deals with this decision."

Halfway through, Richard began to weep uncontrollably. Then he got up and burst out of the room. My heart was pounding so hard I thought my chest would explode. Fear overcame me as my mind raced back to the scene at the junkyard when I was 20 years old. Richard had been angry with me. I was going to move out of his home. He was watching a junkyard for a friend. It was dark, and we were back among all of the junk vehicles. He had a pistol. Why I went along, I don't know. One thing for sure, I have always remembered the unspoken message of power Richard had over me that night, instilled by fear.

His counselor got up and followed him. They never returned, so my counselor and I got up and went back to his office.

Now I didn't know what to expect. I was expecting revenge. Our meeting was in the afternoon, and I went back to work afterwards. I was the only one working late to make up for the time missed that afternoon. It was about 6:00 P.M. The office phone rang. It was my daughter, Tammi, calling to tell me they had just received a call from Richard. He seemed out of control and hysterical.

Richard asked for Terri and said to her, "Did you know Mom's divorcing me?" Terri replied, "Yes." Richard said, "I just want you to know I love you very much and always will. It's not your fault. It's my fault. I'm the one that has the problem. I love you very much!! I love you so much. Nobody knows how much. I hate myself for doing that." Tammi had been listening to Richard and said to him, "Don't do anything to hurt yourself!" He replied, "I will love you no matter what happens."

Well, needless to say, this only prompted the girls to be afraid for Richard's own safety—and theirs. They were frantic by the time they called me.

I called the mental health center and then the police to report the incident. I told them I was afraid for myself and the children's safety. I arranged for a friend to pick up the children and take them to her home. Then I had another friend meet me outside my office and walk with me to my car. I did not know what action Richard would take next, and I wasn't taking any chances. The knife was turning and twisting deep in my gut again.

The police picked him up at his home where he had passed out from drinking. They also confiscated a gun. He spent the night in jail, and got out the next morning.

I was a few weeks into a new job. My life was now starting to make positive changes, but I was still feeling Richard encompassing my life. Each child was struggling to work through their own feelings. Waves of depression, anger, and hopelessness flooded our household. I wasn't sure how we were making it through this period of our lives. I just wanted it all to stop.

Part of my therapy was a wives' support group. Each woman in the group was married or involved in a relationship with a sex offender. These women became the most important support system in my life. We cried together, laughed together, called one another sometimes in the middle of the night, just to cry or say, "I can't sleep. Please talk to me." I read books to help me better understand the reason for incest to happen in my family. I read and read until I was sick of reading about children being hurt.

Time was running short for Richard. Our divorce was final on January 31, 1986. I was extremely relieved it was over! The marriage was over, but not the dynamics of dealing with Richard. Holding a job was impossible for him. He continued to write NSF checks, tell lies, and manipulate people, including his family. As summer approached, he was spending time with Richie, which only caused Richie to vent his anger and frustration at me. For the time being, I was the bad guy in Richie's eyes. He knew that when he was younger Mom always tried to fix things. So why couldn't she now? If only Mom could have believed that Dad would be different and never do that to the girls again, then we could be a family. Of course, Mom couldn't do that. She knew the risk too well!

Richard became very delinquent with his therapy bill. He had been warned he might get kicked out of the sex offender program if he didn't make a substantial payment and arrangements. Dealing with Richard was not any better than before. I could not trust him.

Shadows
Shadows that follow me
wherever I may be.
Haunt my mind;
too confused to find
the answer—where it may lie
hard as I may try.

September 11, 1986—Richard was sentenced to ten years in prison for molesting the girls. Richie spent every day that week until the sentencing hearing with his father. It was a traumatic day for all of us. Emotions flooded my soul, more so than I ever realized could happen. It was similar to the beginning of all of this—not knowing how to feel, what emotion should take precedent: Compassion or anger, love or hate. They all play such an important role in this complicated family crime. How unfortunate to have taken place in our family.

Once I realized it was not easy dealing with Richard going to prison, I was able to come to grips with myself again as I had many times in the past two years.

Like any bit of news, this made the paper. Fortunately the paper was discreet, one small sentence and the victims not mentioned. Whew!! We are through it. I don't think very many people read it.

Richard was in prison. The children were doing better. I had been in and out of a few relationships. The current one was going well. We all felt better about our lives.

Then one day about two or three months after Richard's sentencing hearing, it was discovered that Richard had impersonated his brother, who was chief of police in a neighboring town, before he was sentenced. He used his brother's identity to spend $4,000 on a satellite dish, VCR, and other appliances all on credit. His brother pressed charges, and Richard was taken from prison back to the county jail to await trial on these new charges. I took Richie to visit his father while in town. He seemed to blame his brother for pressing charges, not realizing that's exactly what he should be doing. Richard received another year in prison in addition to the previously sentenced ten.

About one week after Richard's sentencing, I was sitting at my desk at work when I received a phone call. The woman on the other end was very disturbed and angry. It was a voice I knew very well, a member of the support group that I had become especially close to. She said, ''Have you read the paper?'' Of course I hadn't. I was at work. Teresa informed me that I wouldn't like what I read, and that they did a story on Richard impersonating his brother. I got off the phone and went right out and bought a paper. My knees were weak, my stomach in knots, and I just wanted to throw up as I started looking for the article.

There it was on the front page of the second section. The headline read, ''Felon allegedly masquerades as his policeman brother.'' Before the story really started, they gave a run-down on why Richard was in prison. It read, ''Miller is serving ten years in prison for sexual assault charges for molesting his children.''

I was furious, humiliated, embarrassed to think the whole town was going to read this. This very act of a journalist's insensitivity and sensationalism led to a lengthy dialogue with the newspaper. The end results are in a memo the managing editor sent to all the employees:

"To: Newsroom Staff

"A small, three-letter word slipped onto our news pages Thursday that is causing a large amount of pain and anger to some residents.

"The word is an out-and-out mistake on our part and I have apologized, face-to-face and in no uncertain terms, to the mother of the three children who are being badly hurt by those three letters.

"The three-letter word is "his." In a story about recent criminal charges against a man, we printed that he was in prison on earlier 'sexual assault charges for molesting his children.'

"It is our strict policy to never identify victims of rape and child abuse (unless somehow victims want us to identify them in their own self-interest). There is just no justification for making public their identities, in light of the suffering it could cause them.

"Well, in the sentence above, we might as well have used the kids' names, because the kids began getting phone calls from friends, and some pretty nasty crank calls, too, filled with obscenities. Up until now, there were few people who knew that the people who were sexually assaulted were his kids.

"The mother came to see me this afternoon, and I had a long, rather tearful talk with her. She was very reasonable about it, but also very angry and very hurt. The daughters who were molested are freshman and sophomore in high school. A twelve-year-old son was not molested, but now everyone will think he is among those who were, the mother said. All the kids seem pretty devastated, she said, adding that they've all been in counseling, therapy, and court over the original crime the past two years and 'were just starting to pull out of it and be happy again.'

"I won't go on about what else she said because I'm sure you got my point long ago. It's hard for me to tell her how badly this has damaged us and the paper in the eyes of the readers who caught our error. The worst and most frustrating thing is there is no way we can correct our mistake, no way we can try to make things better without exposing those kids further and making it worse.

"Let this be a lesson about our Number One guideline: simple human sensitivity, about all things, no matter how small, and about all people.

"It is absolutely no defense for us to say, 'Well, it is a matter of public record since it was on a court document,' or 'You should be blaming the molester, not the newspaper.' One reason a community lets us be its newspaper is because we serve its needs, on a very personal basis, as much or more than we serve our own.

"We broke no law in this case, the mother's lawyer told her as much, I think, because she came here knowing that she probably doesn't have grounds to sue. She would like—very, very badly—to sue us. I don't blame her a bit. She wishes there were a law to prevent such insensitivity by a newspaper, and I'm not ready to say there shouldn't be. I assured her that our 'guideline' has the force of law in this newsroom. We must all work hard to enforce it.

"I think everyone in this newsroom is sensitive, that we bend over backwards to be, that our sensitivity shows in many of the very stories we choose to write. In the present case, no one was intentionally trying to hurt anyone—a little word slipped through with the deadline pressure. The mother believes that, I think, and she knows no one up here does such things out of cruelty.

"I asked her to please convey our feelings to her children. She asked if I might possibly meet with the children and talk to them about it, too. I said I would be happy to if the children wished it. They don't need our counseling—we need theirs.

"There is no better counselor than a victim.

"In the meantime, the whole newsroom staff will have a meeting on the subject of sensitivity. All I ask is that you be careful and caring out there."

This did not take away the flood of emotions we had come back to haunt us because of one person's lack of compassion; but it did our hearts good to walk in to the newspaper and have them listen to our hurt, and acknowledge their mistake. It has been standing up and fighting for ourselves in these kind of situations that have given us strength and hope for the future.

Richard appealed his prison sentence to the Supreme Court. The paper read:

"Richard A. Miller, who in 1986 pleaded guilty in a plea-bargain to one count of sexual assault and was sentenced to ten years in prison, claims the prosecutor had a conflict of interest in the case.

"Before becoming a deputy county attorney, he had worked in private practice with Miller's defense lawyer, who was familiar with Miller's case and file. The prosecutor's familiarity with Miller prejudiced the attorney against him, according to court papers filed by Miller.

"In addition, Miller claims facts about his criminal history were misrepresented at his sentencing hearing, and that a pre-sentence investigation didn't show that four prior charges had been dismissed or reduced.

"Additionally, Miller claims he was threatened by counselors at Mental Health Services, Inc. who allegedly told him he wouldn't qualify for community based sex offender treatment unless he pleaded guilty and obtained a deferred prison sentence.

"Miller claims the county attorney's office had indicated it wasn't going to prosecute the case, according to the documents."

The reduced prison sentence was denied.

Now serving his time in prison, he is no longer in the sex offender treatment program there. He never completed the program. The judge required during sentencing that the sex offender program must be completed. It appears he will not be going back into therapy for the very reason he is in prison. Sad but true, our legal system, which seemed to be serving justice in our case, has ultimately failed. In 1992, this man will be walking our streets again. My fear is still fresh, afraid of a convicted pedophile who is not getting the much needed treatment ordered by the judge.

We're now going into the fall of 1989. Work is abundant. The children aren't children anymore. They are growing up, learning to be responsible adults.

My own inner struggles are many. Forgive Richard? I told him I could, but I'm resolved to the fact that God will have to handle that for me. I want the best for my family, but cannot fill all their needs. That is difficult for me to accept.

Richie visits his father in prison every four to six weeks for one and a half hours. Richie is undergoing therapy himself now, as he learns to cope and deal with the unhealthy family dynamics we lived with for so long. He still struggles to have a good relationship with his father, knowing it may never come true.

Tammi is married with a darling daughter.

Terri is a senior in high school, struggling to make it, and currently working part-time.

We all have our good and bad days. We try to be open with one another, and we all know that we care very much for each other. The most meaningful way we show each other we care is by just being there, through the good and the bad, and knowing that we will always love each other.

Writing my story has been therapeutic, as I have been flooded with all of the emotions I felt while living this story. Again, I cried, uncontrollably. I hated far more than I ever thought possible. I hurt, an ache no one could comfort. Anger attacking my whole being, self-destructive, the most dangerous, threatening emotion I've ever experienced.

Again, I felt helpless, out of control. Except this time, I was only remembering, not living the emotions anymore. Now hope engulfed my emotions. I still cry, but now hope dries my tears. I still get angry. I have hope this will lessen with time. The hurt is deeply embedded. Hope is the mortar that slowly repairs my broken heart.

Hope

Shadows that haunt me are fading away.
Replaced with Hope for each new day.
Hope that the shadows will one day be
No longer the darkness encompassed by me.
Fading away to haunt me no more.
Hope has opened the door.

You have read about our lives as I have lived it. Now share in Tammi's story as written by her:

✳ ✳ ✳

I can't remember the first time my father approached me, but I was a little girl, I do know that. My father had his ways of coming to me and asking me. He would usually ask me if I wanted something, and then tell me I could have it if I gave him what he wanted. Most of the time he would say okay if I said no, and then later that day or night, he would force me.

When I was about seven, he told me I wasn't his real daughter. I was so relieved that I wasn't part of him (scumbag!).

I hated him ever since I can remember. He wasn't part of our family, and I wanted him to die. I wished he wouldn't have ever married my mom. Then it would just be me and my mom, and I wouldn't have to be afraid of him. He ruined mine and my sister's life by violating our rights. He would come to me and tell me I was beginning to look more like a woman every day. That scared me. I thought to myself, "It's going to get worse and worse the more I grow up."

One time I was sleeping on the couch because I was sick. My sister was upstairs (that's where our bedroom was), and downstairs was a lot warmer. I was scared to death that he would come and hurt me. I kept praying that he would just stay in his room, but I could tell he wouldn't. I could see it in his eyes. I tried to fall asleep, and after a couple hours or so I finally did, because I figured he would let me sleep if he saw I was. The next thing I remember is him on top of me. He kept telling me he wasn't going to hurt me, but it was too late. He started to do things to me I hated with a passion, things like feeling me all over. By then I was crying because it hurt and I was so scared. Then he started to rub his penis on me. He told me he wasn't putting it in, but I wasn't sure because I was a virgin and didn't know what it felt like, and didn't want to know. After he was done, he just got up and left. I was so scared I was shaking, and I wanted to die. I felt like dirt.

Things like that happened a lot through the years. I started to hate my mom for not saving me and protecting me from him. I was always told that every dad did this to his daughter, and he did it because he loved me. I never thought my sister had it done to her. When I found out, I wanted to kill my dad. I wished he would have done it all to me instead of her. I felt so much hate for him. How could he do that to her? She always was so cute and just a little girl. I wanted to take her to a totally different place and start all over again. We could do it, but I knew that wasn't the right thing to do. Plus I couldn't leave my mom. She was a big help when I needed someone to talk to.

My dad left the house on October 31. My sister told. It was Halloween and I was going to go to a party. I was walking down the hall with my best friend. We were going to go to lunch, when I saw my sister walking down the hall. She was crying. I walked over to her and asked her what was wrong. She was crying too hard, so I took her in the bathroom so we could talk in private. She told me, ''Dad, he has been touching me in places he's not supposed to.'' I could feel myself falling apart inside. She was crying, and I hated to see her cry. All I kept thinking was that I was going to kill him. I hated him for what he did to her. Then she asked me if I had it happen to me. I told her yes. Then we just held each other.

After that a teacher came and told me they wanted to talk to her. Well, I thought, ''Fuck them. It's not their little sister.'' But they didn't care. All they wanted was a good paycheck.

They took her, and I went back to lunch. On the way there, I saw my parents. I wondered if that was the reason they were here, but how could they know so soon?

After lunch, I decided to go to the school counselor. I knocked on the door. I only wanted to know where my little sister was. I didn't want to know if the whole world knew my gross secret I had kept for as long as I can remember. He opened the door and said, ''Come on in.'' I sat down, not saying a word, and not planning to. He told me without having to ask that he was going to go get Terri. I still didn't say a word, just shook my head as in yes. He left, leaving me alone. I looked around, looking at all of the pictures that were in his office. ''Boy,'' I thought, ''life is full of ups and downs.'' I wondered sitting there if other people thought life was the most painful thing next to pain. Then I remembered what my little sister had told me. She was one of the people like me, the unlucky ones.

I must have sat there for at least thirty minutes. I remember thinking a lot of things when I was there. I thought that I would try and think of what I was going to say to Terri. First I thought I would tell her how everything was going to be okay, and we'd make it through together. But then I thought what if they won't let us be together?

Then they came in. I looked at my sister and I wanted to cry. She was my lifetime friend ever since she was born. The first thing the counselor said was he wanted to know if we were hungry. And I was. I didn't eat at lunch. My sister sat next to me, and we talked like nothing was wrong. I guess we did that to get our minds off things. But all I could think about was that it happened to her, too. That day was a very confusing day for both of us.

We went to welfare the next day. We both made tapes for them. After everything was out for a while, things started to get better. No more being scared that my father would come into my room in the middle of the night and hurt me. But I did find myself staring at the door, thinking this was all a dream, and thinking he was going to walk in any minute. The more time went on, the stronger I got. And the more guys pushed me around, the more I realized that I don't have to be the way I used to be. I was my own person now, not my father's.

Searching For Support,
Searching For Understanding

Dear God, guide my hand, help me heal.

Between my two jobs one day, I stopped at a store to look around. I had no intentions of buying anything. Thoughts of my daughter would not leave me. She was at home with her two younger brothers, and my cousin was babysitting. I hated working two jobs. I felt so guilty because of the time spent away from my children. I ended up buying my daughter a curling iron before leaving the store and going on to my second job.

Child care has always been a sore subject with me anyway. I constantly worried that something would happen to the kids, especially my daughter. I had sound reasons for my worry. As a child myself, my parents would leave my brothers and me in the care of our uncle, my mom's brother. They felt that we were in trusted hands. I soon learned he could not be trusted. Every time he watched us, he sexually abused me. I soon learned his pattern and feared my parents leaving. Since my daughter's birth, I have feared something like this would happen to her. I watched how men touched her. I listened to how they talked to her. I felt I had some insight. The only problem was that I could not be with her all the time.

Driving home that day, I was not prepared for what I saw or heard. "Mommy, remember what happened to you? It just happened to me." She didn't have to say any more. My heart stopped, my mind raced. By who? "My brother? Oh, God, not my brother?" "No, your cousin." There was no disbelief, no denial. I knew it was true by the terror on her precious face. I filled with rage and ran out the door. My daughter ran after me crying, "No, mommy, no." He had threatened her. I wanted to get my hands on him. I wanted to kill him. I wanted him to feel the terror that my daughter was feeling. I wanted to be the one to cause that terror.

He was not home. Neither were his parents. I turned my attention back to my daughter. I wanted and needed to know that she was all right. I rushed her to the emergency room.

My boys were confused. They could not see an injury. They could not see any blood. It seems not only children are like that. Because people don't see physical scars or bleeding, they think there is no damage.

I was not ready for what was about to happen, and neither was my daughter. They gave my nine-year-old daughter a rape test. As I watched my daughter being poked, pricked, plucked, and probed, I felt so much guilt and anguish for her. My tears for her would not stop. The worst was yet to come. They had to sedate her. It took five adults to hold her down to give her a pap smear. I was one of those adults. All the while she's screaming at me. "What are they doing down there? What are they doing to me?" Tears streaming down her face and mine, she looked at me and said, "Mommy, you never went through this. You never had to have this done."

Hours went by. After they pulled hairs from her head, and dug under her nails; after they took spit samples, urine samples, blood samples, and the pap smear; after the doctors, nurses, and detectives entered and exited like butterflies, I carried my sexually-abused, rape-tested, drugged, nine-year-old little girl out into the darkness and the coldness of the night and the world.

I could not take my daughter home that night. Our home no longer felt safe because my cousin, the boy who had forced her to have sexual intercourse, lived only two houses away. We went to my parents' house. They were out of town, but my brother was there with my two boys.

I tried to feed her something because the whole time we were in the emergency room, she begged for something to eat. She was beyond eating now, beyond reality. All she could do was sleep. I was grateful that she slept as I undressed her and put her to bed. I prayed that in her sleep, she would dream of things that nine-year-old little girls dream of. I hoped that she would find peace in her sleep. I felt that night that our mother-daughter bond had become much stronger. We had a mutual knowledge between us, a mutual understanding, and mutual feelings that only come from being sexually abused. I felt such a longing to comfort my daughter and to be comforted. As I held my precious little girl through the night, my mind filled with memories of the nine years past and the uncertain future that awaited us.

The morning came too soon. I could have lain forever in that bed with her, because I could protect her there; I could comfort her and hold her and love her. I remembered how I had done just that when she was just born.

Reality kicked in soon enough. She had to be at the detective's office to make a formal and taped statement. My brother fixed an enormous breakfast for us, but we could not eat. My boyfriend came to get the boys, and my best friend took us to the police station. The detective soon realized that she was still heavily sedated, and asked us to return the next day.

My boyfriend was very supportive for the next few days. He took the boys under his wing and tried to keep normalcy in their lives. I was not capable. It seemed as though my daughter and I had fallen into this deep, dark hole.

The next few days were spent helplessly wandering. The world was not a safe place to live. So we went from house to house and place to place, never feeling safe anywhere or with anyone. I didn't know where to go, who to trust, who cared and who didn't. So many questions, so many feelings, and so many fears plagued me. I was searching for normalcy, searching for some balance, searching for some control. It seemed our lives were in the control of others. The abuser had the control, the justice system had the control, and the Crime Victims Unit had control. All seemed to decide our fate.

I quit one job to be with the children more, especially my daughter. I could not afford to quit, but I felt it gave me the balance I was looking for. Besides that, there were things I could no longer bear to see or hear at that job, things like pornographic magazines kept there by the men and sick jokes about having sex with little girls. If the men saw that they could make my flesh crawl or upset me, they would do it or say it all the more. They found some kind of pleasure in it. Not everyone was like that, but there were a few. They are the ones that made it impossible to go back. Pornographic magazines had caused overwhelming, destructive flashbacks to my own sexual victimization a few years ago.

My life was changing for various reasons, not because I wanted it to, but because of the circumstances. I felt so alone, so afraid. I wanted to run from everything—the fears, the memories of my own abuse, the responsibility of being ''Mommy.'' I felt intense rage for my cousin. I decided to move. I could no longer live there. It was too close for comfort.

I broke my foot moving and spent six weeks in a cast. I was already stressed out and feeling helpless. The cast just made things worse. It was also a bill I couldn't afford.

My relationship with my boyfriend became a nightmare. I was either very angry or very upset all the time. He couldn't handle it. This had not touched his life as it had touched ours. Maybe the difference was that she was not born of his flesh, his blood. He could not understand why we couldn't just put it behind us. Finally he broke up with me. I found myself longing and searching for support, for comfort, and there seemed none to be found anywhere, from anyone.

Then the next thing that happened was that my mother returned to town after a trip and she found out. She was rushed to the hospital. She was devastated. She went back twenty years and thought it was me again. She thought it was her daughter rather than her granddaughter. I had to go to the hospital and show her that I was all right, that it wasn't me. The next day I took my daughter to see her, to show her that she was all right also. What enters my mind the most about her stay in the hospital was the three of us sitting at the table talking, three generations of women traumatized by incest. I found a new understanding towards my mom. We also have a stronger bond between us. I realize now how hard it is for a mother to cope with the fact that her daughter has been sexually abused.

I wrote a letter to the children's father. I felt he had a right to know. I thought that he would want to know. I felt that my daughter needed a loving supportive man in her life to help her heal. I also needed financial help in order to move. In return, I received a horrible letter back, not from him but from his wife. I couldn't believe another woman could not be compassionate. It said that she didn't think it sounded that bad. She cursed me for asking for help. It was a letter of no support, no concern, no understanding. How bad does rape have to be before it's considered bad? That was the question that plagued me. I found so many people minimizing it, treating it like a sore that would go away.

My daughter waited for months to hear from her dad. In the time she waited, both the boys received birthday cards and money from him. She received nothing, and I could see the heartbreak in her eyes. I was so angry with him for turning away from her when she so needed his love, support and understanding.

I turned my hope, my faith, and my eyes to the justice system, only to find that there didn't seem to be any justice. But they constantly assured me that the wheels of justice were turning. Turning toward whom, I'm not sure. I felt my daughter had become just another statistic, another file collecting dust in the dust ball that we call our justice system. I found myself dealing with people who are numb to it all because they have dealt with so much of it. It feels like there was this glass wall between us. They were so impersonal, and I couldn't help but feel very personal. It's a very personal subject.

I feel that they have slapped his hand, called him a bad boy, and put him back on the street. Every time I see him, I feel such anger and betrayal by our justice system. He has only been advised to stay away from us. One day he was after my youngest son trying to scare him. I told him to stay away from my children and that I was calling the county attorney's office. A few days later, I was called into the county attorney's office and was informed that my aunt wanted to press charges against me! They went on to say that because of the circumstances, they would not press charges. Am I supposed to be grateful or what? It was hard to believe they could consider pressing charges against me when the abuser was free to walk the streets.

The court dates were terrible. It was like sitting in on the Hatfields and McCoys, my family sitting on one side, his on the other. The other family members didn't sit anywhere, they just went back and forth. There is a lot of stress in the family now. I'm not really sure who I can talk to sometimes because I don't know if they'll go running back to his family with what I had to say. The family has definitely been torn in half.

I feel bad for my dad because it is his sister, and family ties are very important to my dad. When it first happened, they had words, and I don't think they have spoken since. She told my dad she was going to try to prove that I was an unfit mother. My dad exploded and told her to sweep off her own porch before she starts judging others, and that my children have never been left alone, whereas she leaves her boys alone all the time and has for years. No one ever said that this was going to be easy. She has never pursued the matter any further.

My daughter and I began therapy, and after the therapist saw my daughter twice, she said my daughter was doing fine and no longer needed to be seen. More harsh realities followed.

My daughter was doing so fine that she was sexually abused again, this time by a trusted friend. Believe me, I had monitored this boy. I had watched him with her. After everything we had been through, who wouldn't? He was my best friend's stepson. I had spoken with the friend about the sexual abuse. She and her husband reassured me that they had talked to him and that he would never do anything like that. He had been raised properly.

This time my daughter didn't tell me, my youngest son did. He had walked in on them. I confronted my daughter and she told me that nothing had happened, and I let it go. I needed to think. I knew something had happened by the fear on her face. Part of me didn't want to believe it. Part of me wanted to say okay, she says nothing happened, I can say nothing happened. Not again. Please, God, not again.

By this time, my boyfriend was back in our life again. Our breakup lasted three weeks. He needed time to cool off because being with me could be like working with dynamite. He had come to my house that day to get me to go shopping for school supplies for the kids.

He knew something was wrong and suggested that we go for a ride. I did not expect to hear from him what I did. My insides cried out, "No, not from him, too!" I told him what my son and daughter had told me that morning. In all his logic and intelligence, with his degree and so-called knowledge of the world, he told me that this kept happening because of my financial status. "Well, it's not like you're the president of IBM." And, of course, it was my influence on her. Surely she was using her sexuality to get what she wanted. In other words, he was calling my nine-year-old little girl a slut.

I was already a loaded gun and he just pulled the trigger. He also became the target. Doesn't this man know that rape happens in rich neighborhoods, too, that no influence, no set of moral teachings or values matter? Not for the victim, anyway. If there is a rapist or an abuser out there, he will rape and abuse. He will use any tactics, any skills, any force that he has. The first incident was by force, the second manipulation. I could not believe that this man was attacking our character and blaming us.

There was only emotion to follow. I was already questioning myself and my responsibility.

I went home and shut myself off. I cried and cried. Every word he spoke sunk into my heart and my mind. "Maybe he's right. Maybe it is all my fault. Maybe I have raised her wrong. Maybe, maybe, maybe . . ." No, I would not take responsibility for this. I carried the responsibility for my own incest for too many years.

I put the kids in the car and drove to his house. I was not going to lay down my guns, I was going to fight. When I got to his house, I did a lot of yelling at him.

Then I went to the boy's house and confronted him and his parents. All I remember was asking him, "How could you? How could you do this? I trusted you," I screamed. His dad looked at him and said, "You're dead." I left, but I was still loaded with ammunition.

The boy's parents called the police and told them what had happened. The police began looking for us. When they found us, the police wanted us to go to the police station and again make a formal statement. I refused for my daughter's sake. She told me she didn't want to go through it all again. I understood and respected her wishes.

The next day, I went to my parents' house and my mother looked at me with anger in her eyes. No one had told her that her granddaughter had been sexually abused again. She thought that I had just had another fight with my boyfriend. I needed her so badly. I needed a hug from my mom, but there was just her anger. She finally realized something more was going on when the police kept calling and I kept taking my daughter into the other room to talk to her after each phone call. Finally she asked me what was going on and I told her in tears. My daughter would not talk to me or my mother, and that tore at my heart. I couldn't understand why. Later a woman from Child Protective Services called, and I agreed that I would bring my daughter in to see her the next day. If she talked, she talked. If she didn't, she didn't. I was not going to force her or push her.

That night I went home and my mother's angry eyes haunted me. My boyfriend's words haunted me. What these two boys had done to my daughter haunted me, and fear of what I would hear tomorrow haunted me. My heart felt shattered for so many reasons and by so many people. I didn't know if I could go on. I didn't know if I wanted to go on. This world was too cruel, too ugly.

The next day also came too soon. All I wanted to do was sleep. Please, God, just let me sleep. No, I had to get up and take my daughter to Child Protective Services. The boy had already made his statement. When we got there, the lady tried to get my daughter to talk and she wouldn't. So the woman repeated what the boy had said happened and my daughter agreed. I could not believe it. My nine-year-old daughter had sexual intercourse again. No, God, not again. I can't go through this again. She can't go through this again. Why is this happening?

When I got home, I just couldn't cope, so I had my son call my mom and she came over right away. When I got home, there was a note on the door from my boyfriend. He was not concerned about my daughter; he was not concerned about me; he was not apologizing for all of the hateful things he had said. His only concern was for two movies he had rented and left at our house. He wanted me to return them. Can someone return my child's innocence, please? Can someone return her virginity? Can someone, anyone, be loving, concerned and kind?

When my mom got there, I just broke down and cried. Oh, the movies. Must return the movies. Forget that my daughter has been sexually abused again. All he cares about is his damn movies. I returned his movies to him and he even said thank you. I couldn't help it. I just began yelling at him, screaming at him. All he could say was that he was no longer going to take my verbal abuse. There is nothing worse than crying out and being ignored. Nothing worse than reaching out and having your hand slapped down. Yet I was becoming quite used to it.

When I returned home, my mother was gone. She didn't know how to help me, what to do for me. I could relate to that because I didn't know what to do to help my daughter either. My self-esteem was at ground zero. I questioned every part of me. It had to be me. There was something wrong with me. I was an emotional live wire, and every fiber stood on end. Waiting to be touched. No one ever knew how I was going to act or react.

That night, my brother stayed with us. I went to my room and closed myself off. I no longer knew what to do as a person or as a mother. Whatever my lifeline was had just been cut. I searched my heart, my soul, my mind for answers, for direction. There was none to be found.

The next day should have been an exciting day. It was the first day of school—a day filled with the clatter of their excitement, the clatter of their feet and their mouths as they prepared for a beginning of new friendships, new growth. I only waited for them to leave so that I could leave. I found no joy in their clatter. I was immobile. I knew I had to do something, to talk to someone. I dressed, went downstairs, and told my brother that I was going to talk to someone.

I went to the mental health center and was seen right away. I broke down and couldn't stop shaking. I was admitted to the hospital. I finally found what I was looking for, a floor full of people that would just listen to me. Listen to me yell, scream, cry. They were compassionate, concerned, and understanding. They gave me hope, guidance, and direction. They gave me insight and support.

The day I left the hospital, I had to stop and get some things at the drug store. I thank God that I was with my mother because I ran into one of the abusers (the friend). My mom just grabbed me and held me tight. I never know when I might run into my uncle, my cousin, my daughter's ex-friend.

When I got home, there were more emotional scars. My daughter felt responsible for me being in the hospital. My oldest son withdrew from me. My youngest began wetting his bed and turned to his sister for mothering. All expressed to me their fear of me leaving and never coming back. So there was more building to be done. I was stronger. I hated myself for my weakness. I missed all of the supportive people at the hospital. I still had a lot of feelings that needed to be dealt with. I took a few days to get back in the swing of things and then returned to work. It only lasted two days, and then I was laid off. Another landslide in an active avalanche. So many losses, so many changes, so much to cope with.

The hardest part of all of this is seeing my nine-year-old daughter in all of her innocent and youthful ways, and then seeing the reality of how much pain there has been in just seven short months. There is no minimizing it. There is no pretending or acting like it didn't happen when I have to monitor my daughter so she won't be sexually assaulted again, when my son and daughter can no longer sleep together in an innocent manner. The innocence has been robbed. It is gone forever. No, there is no minimizing it when there seems to be no justice. There is no minimizing it when the two boys who sexually abused her are still on the street. There is no minimizing it when our society seems to accept sexual abuse and minimize the effects caused by it.

I had mentioned at the beginning that I had bought my daughter a curling iron. I still wonder why I bought it, but I think I know why. I think mothers and their children have this glorious bond, a bond of the hearts, the souls, the spirit. My daughter was crying out to me that day and I heard her. It will take a lot more than a curling iron or any material object to bring her happiness or make up for what's been done to her.

I wish I had the strength and the courage that she seems to have. I have read a lot about sexual abuse and its effects. One of the things I read is that a little girl is not able to cope or understand what has happened to her, so she separates herself from it. She pushes it down, deep, deep down. That is exactly what I did. But I also learned that it comes back. It comes back to the surface.

I guess that I am grateful that both incidents were isolated. I am very proud that both my son and daughter found the courage to tell me. My daughter is getting the help that she needs. Hopefully with that help, this will not have a dramatic effect on her throughout her life. This is what I pray for. As far as myself, I have lost a lot of trust and a lot of faith. We are now living on unemployment, for as long as that lasts.

A lot of people who used to come around don't come around anymore. My boyfriend is a part of the past since I found out that he had a fourteen-year-old son that he has never acknowledged. I'm stressed out most of the time. I have lost twenty pounds in the seven months since all of this started. I couldn't tell you how much sleep I've lost, but anyone can tell by the dark circles under my eyes. I fear and question my sexuality, my mothering, and my personhood. I also fear and question everyone else. I feel as my daughter must have the night she got the rape test. I feel poked, pricked, plucked, and probed. There is not one fiber of my being that has not been touched by this. I have had people come right up to me and say that I let my daughter be raped.

I wonder how much endurance one is supposed to have. I fear going back to work. I fear leaving my children with anyone, and my children fear me leaving them.

So our search continues, our search for normalcy, our search for trust, and our search for compassionate, caring, loving people who do not turn their backs when we are in a crisis. We are on the road to recovery. We have a lot of healing to do. Our hearts have a lot of mending to do. I pray that the worst is behind us. I think it's very important that the mother and child both have a good, strong support system. We need to be able to express all that we are feeling, our anger, rage, our tears and fears. We need a silent partner; someone who will listen to us without judging, minimizing or blaming; a person that for that hour or two or three or four, will listen without turning and walking away. We need love and support.

Recently I found myself turning back to God for that love and that support because I couldn't find it anywhere else. He is the only silent partner that I can seem to find. I'm not even sure that He is there, but I talk to Him and He does not interrupt me. He does not look at his watch because He has lost interest and patience with what I have to say, or because He's in a hurry. He does not turn away when I scream and cry. I find a peace with God as my silent partner. But it would be nice to get a hug occasionally, or to have someone hold my hand, or to look into the eyes of someone who really loves me and understands me. My daughter finds all those things in me, but I am still searching.

So where we're going, I don't know. What will be the outcome for us? I don't know. Where are all those people that I thought cared about us? I don't know. What will happen to those boys? I don't know. We are still searching. My Silent Partner is at my side, and as my guide.

God grant me the serenity to accept the things I cannot change, the courage to change the things I can, and the wisdom to know the difference.

Can anyone ever really accept that our children, God's children, are being sexually abused? I am still searching for that acceptance.

I curse myself constantly because I wasn't stronger and because I didn't handle things better. I find myself always saying, "Maybe if I had done this or that, things would have turned out differently."

I was not prepared for this. I handled it the best I could at the time. I wasn't prepared for all the harsh realities that faced me. I wasn't prepared to be teaching my children about sex at the young ages that they were. I wasn't prepared for my six-year-old's question the day he came up to me and asked me what rape was. I wasn't prepared for all of the different reactions that I was hearing and seeing from all of the different people, all of the different perspectives from which people see this. It is like looking through a kaleidoscope, where one minute your vision seems clear, and the next minute everything is changing. I feared waking up in the morning because I never knew what the day would bring; I never knew what feelings and memories of my own abuse would surface. My daughter is the victim, but it has affected the lives of many. I don't think anyone will walk away from this without its mark on them somehow, some way.

There are two people I have not mentioned very much. Those two people are my sons. I wonder what marks it has left on them. They have been on an emotional ride, not because they wanted to go for that ride, but because they were there. It's like they have been taken through a zoo where their mother rushes them from one cage to another. One minute they are looking at the lions and tigers. The next minute they are looking at the monkeys and then at the reptiles. Their world has also been turned inside out. I picture them asking me, "Why are we going through this zoo? One minute we are looking at the mean, angry animals, and the next minute we are looking at chaotic, crazy ones, and then the sleazy, slimy ones." That is what our world has been like for the last seven months. I keep taking them through this zoo hoping to find the soft, tender animals who bring harm to no one. They stay within their cages and live their lives without bothering anyone or anything. My boys are tired of this zoo. They want to go home so they can play games with their friends, and do all of the normal things that they are supposed to be doing.

My loneliness absorbs me. When I see a TV program on sexual abuse or read about it in a newspaper or a magazine and the lives it has touched, I get scared all over again. I fear going outside my doors. I fear letting my daughter go out. She does not seem to carry the fear that I do. Her life is back to normal. I hate it. I can't stand this fear. I can't stand the power it seems to have over me.

All I know is I am scared for the parents and the children. I am angry at the abusers who perpetrate sexual offenses and try to justify them. Our society has to change. Our justice system has to change. I think the women are going to have to bring these changes on. We have to pull together and show the abusers just how powerful we are and give them something to fear.

✳ ✳ ✳

"Dear Mom:

I think you are doing great. I am sure everyone else thinks you are doing great, too. I am grateful for you. I am glad you are doing this, Mom. It might help us, and might help us for what has happened to us. Your story is great. It's terrific. It's fabulous. I love it."

A MOTHER'S LOVE

Can a mother's love ever be strong enough, giving enough, understanding enough to help her?
To guide her, protect her, shelter her.

As she grows, her pain deepens, and I feel it's harder to reach her. Harder to hold her, guide her, protect her.

A mother's love can be a helpless love.

Helpless as to what to do for her to help her pain subside.
I feel a distance from her that I have never felt before.
I see her moving into the lonely world of isolation.
The same world that I walked in for so long.

A mother's love can be a painful love.

My heart grieves for her, and I want to pull her out of the world of isolation, because I know what a painful world that can be.

A mother's love is a patient love.

As my daughter walks this lonely path, I must be patient. I can walk beside her and hold her hand and pray that somewhere along her path she will open up and let all her feelings, her thoughts, her pain flow out.

A mother's love is a lonely love.

I feel a loneliness as I walk beside her, for there is a part of her that I no longer know, a part of her that she isn't ready to reveal.

A mother's love is an accepting love.

I must accept that my daughter is not ready to talk, and continue this helpless, painful, patient, lonely, and accepting path that a mother walks.

WALK, MY CHILD

When love feels bitter, distant and cold.
Walk.
Walk along a mountain side, feel the wind brush your face.
Know that I am with you. I am love.
As you walk, think.
Think about loving arms that reach out to hold you and keep you warm, when life seems so cold.
As the sun shines down upon you, think about a smile, my smile, a smile that warms your heart and takes your cares away.
You can do it, my child.
When you walk in the bitter cold, you can feel all the warmth and love inside.
Think of me, my child.
Think of love.

It doesn't matter the season or the changes that life brings.
It doesn't matter how cruel life seems to be.
Walk my child and think of me.
For I, my child, love you and will always love you.

I took a walk one night, my child.
I had left you in the care of someone else, to shed myself from some of the pain that I feel, to possibly laugh a little, to forget my troubles. I left you, my child, to spend time with somebody that I loved and cared for.
Sitting across the table, there was no laughter, no love, no concern.

I took a walk, my child, and I thought of you.
It was bitter cold and dark, and I was so scared.
I thought of you, my child.
I cried, my child, because all the love I would ever need was with you, and I had left you in the care of someone else.
I felt guilt, my child.
I continued to walk, and I felt such warmth thinking of you.
I thought of your laughter and your smiles, and your tears, and I realized that all the love I would ever need was with you.

Walk, my child, and in the whispers of the wind, hear me calling out that I love you.
Walk, my child, and in the bitterness of the cold, know that I am there to warm you.
Walk, my child, and in the sun's rays, know that I am with you and see my smile.
Walk, my child, and in the pouring rain, know that it is the tears that I have cried for you.
Walk, my child, and know that I am with you.
And always remember that I have walked, too.

About the Author

Sandi Ashley, Ed.S., is a Licensed Professional Counselor in private practice. She specializes in treatment of survivors of sexual assault and their families. She also consults with foster parent groups and inpatient treatment centers helping them establish a program emphasis for treatment of sexually abused children. She is a member of the community child protection team.

Ms. Ashley holds a B.S. degree in psychology from Colorado State University, and an Ed.S. degree in school psychology from the University of Kansas.

In 1982, she began her career as a family counselor. She then joined the newly created Sexual Assault Treatment Program of Mental Health Services, Incorporated. As a psychotherapist, she provided individual, group and family therapy for perpetrators and survivors of sexual assault. One of her most satisfying endeavors was establishing a therapy group for mothers of incest survivors.

Ms. Ashley lives in Helena, Montana with her husband and two teenage children.